# Writing Murder

## A Basic Guide to Writing Mystery Novels

### Edited by S.M. Harding

Writing Murder
A Basic Guide to Writing Mysteries

Edited by S. M. Harding

978-0-9849501-0-2

INwords, The Writers' Center of Indiana
Indianapolis, Indiana

# Writing Murder

## A Basic Guide to Writing Mystery Novels

### Edited by S.M. Harding

**The Writers' Center of Indiana**

Writers' Center of Indiana,
Indianapolis

WRITING MURDER

ISBN 978-0-9849501-0-2

# Introduction

The roots of this book were a series of writing classes held at The Mystery Company in Carmel, Indiana and co-sponsored by the Writer's Center of Indiana. The more remote cause was the number of people who came into the store looking for advice on writing and publishing crime novels. The series, called Writing Murder, was offered in 2007 and 2008 with 17 mystery authors as faculty. We would like to thank each author and every student for their enthusiastic participation.

Writing is like following the strands of a spider web. Each filament is separate, yet they crisscross and it takes every one to make the whole strong. So, you will find the following essays often weave in a strand from another. Sometimes, there may be conflicting advice, which is fine because none of these writers want to have their essays quoted like the Bible. We've included chapters on setting, scene, character, plot, dialogue, voice, point of view, and pacing – all of the basic elements of writing. In addition, you will find areas on the mystery genre, research, what to do when the manuscript is finished, and several essays on breaking into the industry.

As you read, be alert for variations on the following themes: Agency, Tension, Believability, and Superflux.

*Agency* means your writing is active, not passive. This applies from using active voice in verb choice to a protagonist who keeps moving toward her goal regardless of obstacles.

*Tension* is crucial to plot. If the reader isn't asking "what happens next?" he won't turn the page. Tension isn't used in the plot alone, but also in characters' internal and external competing choices or the way the setting is described.

While a plot must be *believable*, so must the culture, place, and character motivations. It is tempting to use characters like pieces on a chess board, but if the reader is shaking her head and asking why, you've lost her.

*Superflux* simply means too much: too much back story, too much meaningless dialogue, too much technical information, too much detail that isn't important.

Several of our authors have described mystery novels flying across the room. Not from some paranormal phenomena, but rather through a reader's frustration, loss of patience, or disgust. And yes, in my younger years I remember flinging a few; now, I just stop reading. Why? Because the writer took a shortcut, took the easy way out, wrote something implausible – in other words, didn't care. They didn't write with the care or passion they expect the reader to have. If you're writing a crime novel to make money and it seems easy, forget it. The business of publishing is rapidly changing: publishing houses have consolidated, all sorts of e-commerce have emerged in the past few years, and selling in a crowded marketplace means you must have a stellar product. If you're looking for a formula that will land you on the bestsellers' list with a movie deal, there is no such thing.

The only advice most writers give is to find your own unique voice, keep improving your craft, and tell the story that's important to you with passion. That's equally true if you're writing for publication or your own enjoyment.

So sit back, enjoy the different voices of the authors who have contributed to this volume. Then write!

-   S.M. Harding

# A Chalk Outline

# Literary Mysteries: A Contradiction in Terms?
### by Barbara Shoup

Some years ago, I walked into the humanities office at the high school where I was teaching at the time and found a student sitting at a table, a blank sheet of paper in front of him, looking seriously glum.

"What's up?" I asked.

"I have to define what a classic is for World Lit," he said. "I have no freaking *idea.*"

"Hmmm," I said. "Have you seen that movie *Gone in Sixty Seconds*?"

He brightened. "Yeah," he said. "*Awesome* movie."

"Okay. I know you guys saw *To Kill a Mockingbird* in Critical Thinking last year. What about that?"

"Awesome," he said again.

"So. After you saw *Gone in Sixty Seconds*, did you think about it?"

"What do you mean, *think* about it?" he asked.

"Did it stay on your mind? You know, the characters – and what happened to them? The world they lived in?"

He looked at me like I was crazy. "It was a bunch of guys stealing cars," he said.

"Right. What about *To Kill a Mockingbird*? Did you think about that?"

"Yeah. Sometimes I still do." I saw the tiniest flicker of...*something* in his eyes. He thought a moment.

"Uh, classics make you think?"

"Bingo!" I said. "Start there."

I let it go at that. I didn't have the heart to confuse matters by admitting that I didn't really believe there was a be-all and end-all definition for what a classic was – or, worse, share my opinion about academics and critics who all too often believe they have the right to decree which books are classics and which ones are not. Or even what is or isn't just plain literary.

Like literary mysteries: *not*. According to them, the term is an oxymoron. Mysteries are genre fiction – and all genre fiction is, by definition, unworthy to ascend to the high plain of literature.

I beg to disagree.

I think *every* good story is a mystery. Every good story sets characters in motion in a situation that poses a series of logistical and human questions that are crafted to keep the reader turning the pages. What makes any story literary, no matter the genre, is the richness of the fictional world the writer creates on the page, as well as the complexity of the questions he poses and the degree to which the humanity of each character is at stake in their resolution.

The questions Derek Nikita ponders in "What the Hell Is a Literary Thriller, Anyway?" can be applied in assessing the literary qualities of any novel. "Is it workmanlike versus beautiful language, big events and big emotion versus small events and subtle emotion, neatly tied up endings versus endings that require the reader to come to some of his own conclusions that cause critics to categorize one novel as genre and another as literary? Is it subjective, in the eye of the beholder? Is someone who wants to write mysteries obligated to write them the way the majority of readers want them to be written?

"Some of us writers have this crazy whim to shoot for insight and profundity just as much as we want to spin a good yarn," he said. The tone is a little defensive, with the hint of a second, unspoken, question. *Is there something wrong with this?*

Not a thing, in my view. Go for it!

Nonetheless, it's true that most mysteries and thrillers can fairly be categorized as escape fiction. Most novels, *period,* can be categorized that way. They're plot driven, with entertaining, predictable characters, lots of tension cranks, and interesting twists that keep you turning the pages. They're like candy. Addictive, then gone. You move on to the next treat.

But there are also character-driven mystery novels, and those who write them use murder as a lens through which to explore the human experience. Think James Lee Burke, P.D. James, Ruth Rendell. These writers are master plotters who know to sustain the reader's interest in discovering who killed, and why. They know how to bring the logistics of a mystery to a believable and satisfying resolution. But the plots they devise are rooted in the psyche of their characters, and the human questions they raise as the murder investigation unfolds resonate in the reader's mind long after the story is over.

The language they use is beautiful according to Tolstoy's definition: "clarity is beauty." Whether plain, formal, or somewhere in between, it is of a piece with the characters, the setting, the situation, and the nature of the story being told. Their style is as unique and recognizable as, say, the very literary novelist Tim O'Brien – whose *In the Lake of the Woods* is one of the best, most harrowing mystery novels I've ever read – though you won't find it on the mystery shelf. Nor will you find the many, many other literary novels with crime at their core.

I think S.J. Rozan, author of the Bill Smith/Lydia Chin mystery series and several best selling stand-alones, was dead-on when she observed, "There is a need to separate high culture from low culture, especially in this country. If art – high culture, literature – is difficult to comprehend, then only the trained and sensitive and worthy can comprehend it. So the more difficult something is, the more you can congratulate yourself if you get it. Conversely, if everybody gets it and loves it, it cannot, by definition, be art. It's that kind of thinking that puts genre writing, which is beloved by a vast number of people, in the category of not-art. Every now and then, a book rises. I'm thinking of Scott Turow's *Presumed Innocent*, which is a fabulous novel, beautifully written. People said, 'Turow transcends the genre.' Every time you get a book with a crime element that gets a tremendous amount of critical attention, they say that. They take all the cream off the top and then complain that the milk is skim. But that's hardly fair!"

Sadly, this is unlikely to change. Even if critics would finally, rightly agree that there is such a thing as literary mysteries, they'd never be able to agree on a definition. Maybe the real literary mystery is, *Why do we care?* Maybe a better, more useful question for people who love books is, What kind of books fall somewhere between genre and literary novels, and are they worthy of our attention?

Intelligent, serious (generally, not academic) readers will almost certainly agree that the majority of really good books fall somewhere between genre and literary novels and, yes, they are worthy of our attention. They'll also tell you that these in-between books are the ones they most love to read. The closest I can come to defining the books in this category, mainstream or genre, is to say that they have too much depth to be purely commercial, but are too grounded in story, not enough concerned with style to be purely literary. Since the literary world seems dead-set on labels, let's just call them Good Books.

There's a range of Good Books, of course. From Ho-hum Good Books all the way to Really Fabulous Good Books, some of which might even eke their way to the low end of literary on a good day – with a little help from their publishers.

As Nikita said, "I've claimed before that the best fiction is the kind that blurs literary and genre, but that's because I'm a 'literary thriller' writer, according to my press kit."

The *crème de la crème* of Good Books are original and well written, with strong voice and distinctive style – the product of their authors' intense engagement with issues of genuine interest to them. Their plots grow from the lives of complex, often paradoxical characters, and they hinge on issues that are familiar and of concern to "real" people. Their endings are satisfying, but also resonant, allowing the reader to imagine beyond the last pages of the story.

Readers live inside Good Books and, often, carry the characters forever after in their hearts. Good Books can crack open a reader's world; Good Books can (and do) change lives. What writer wouldn't want to write a book that fits this description?

Personally, I cancel all other forms of entertainment when a new Elizabeth George comes out. I never tire of her eclectic ensemble of characters, who grow older and change with each book, just as real people do, and whose lives offer up personal and professional circumstances that she explores by way of intricate plots that keep me turning the pages late at night.

And Michael Connelly's early Harry Bosch? I actually worried about him *between* books; he was that real to me. I love Tony Hillerman's later Joe Leaphorn novels for the way the plots hinge both on the wisdom and physical limitations that age brings.

I still think about the end of S.J. Rozan's *Absent Friends*, a book set in the aftermath of 9/11 – and every single time I do, it breaks my heart.

Reading just doesn't get any better than that.

Perhaps Kevin Guilfoile, posting on the Outfit blog, best delineates the literary/genre distinction: "Suspense novels [mysteries, thrillers, some cozies] explore, again and again, not just the reasons human beings kill each other but, just as significantly, the reasons human beings don't kill each other more often than we do. Almost all suspense fiction is set at the horizon of decency where we've drawn the line representing mankind's ultimate and universal prohibition against taking another person's life. These stories are frequently about the people who seek to cross that line, the individuals assigned to keep them from doing it, and the people who are terrorized and victimized when that ethical wall is breached. The point of it, if I can avoid making it sound too self-important, is to understand what it means to be human. That's the point of all fiction, of course, but suspense novelists have staked out this particular territory on the edge."

In other words, good genre fiction makes you think about that edge.

# Which Team Do I Play For?
## *Identifying Your Subgenre*
### by Dana Kaye

When you write your first book, the last thing you think about is marketing. You focus on characters, setting, and telling a compelling story. You revise scenes, throw away chapters, and rethink plot points. Throughout the writing and rewriting process, do you ever stop to think how a publisher is going to market your book? Not likely.

But when you *complete* your manuscript and begin submitting to agents and publishers, the first thing they will ask you is, "What type of book is it?"

Although the quality of the book is most important to agents and editors, ultimately, it's their job to sell it. They need to have an idea of where the book will be shelved, who will buy it, and which critics will want to review it. Understanding the type of book you have written is a necessary step in the publishing process, and although you may view your creation as indefinable art, in order to sell your book, you must put a label on it.

## Mysteries vs. Thrillers

This is an ongoing discussion in the genre fiction community: what differentiates a mystery from a thriller? Both genres share shelf-space in the bookstore, many authors bear both titles – mystery author, thriller author – and readers often use the terms interchangeably. So what's the difference between the two?

Mysteries are reflective novels. The main crime has already happened or happens within the first twenty pages. The drive of the novel is discovering who committed the crime and why. Sometimes mysteries feature a P.I., cop, or amateur sleuth, but it's not mandatory. The key element in a mystery is that there is a puzzle to be solved.

The driving force of thrillers is something that hasn't happened yet: a bomb is set to explode, someone has a hit on them, or a child has been kidnapped. Thrillers have high-stakes and a risk of impending doom. In mysteries, someone has already been murdered. In thrillers, someone *will* be if the protagonist doesn't stop it.

Obvious examples of each would be Raymond Chandler and Michael Crichton. Or Michael Connelly and James Rollins. If you're even vaguely familiar with their work, you know that Chandler and Connelly are mystery authors while Crichton and Rollins write thrillers. But most novels' genres aren't so apparent. Often times there are many factors driving the story forward and your protagonist has many motivations driving them to act. To clarify things for yourself (and potential agents and editors) ask yourself the following:

> What is the first turning point or first conflict in the novel? Is it something that has already happened or something that is going to happen?

> What are your protagonist's motivations? Are they trying to solve a crime or stop one from taking place? What personal need is driving them to act?

Because "mystery" and "thriller" are such broad terms, there are further classifications given to novels, called subgenres. In addition to helping editors and agents market the book, subgenres assist readers in identifying the types of books they like. John Grisham is famed for his legal thrillers, P.D. James for police procedural mysteries, and Stephen King for paranormal suspense. Fans of these acclaimed authors are more likely to read books with the same subgenre label, but make sure you affix the right label to your novel. You don't want to give agents, editors and readers the wrong impression.

## Mystery Subgenres

Cozy vs. Hard Boiled

Cozies and Hard Boiled novels reside at each end of the mystery spectrum. In cozy mysteries, all of the sex and violence takes place off-stage. Examples include Agatha Christie, Dorothy Sayers, and Nicholas Blake. Most cozies are part of a series, feature an amateur sleuth and often take place in a small town. Current trends include craft cozies in which the protagonist is involved with a craft such as scrapbooking or needlepoint, food cozies which include recipes and foodie tips, and historical cozies which take place during a past time period. Don't let the label fool you, cozies can have just as much tension and suspense as thrillers, but you won't find any blatant sex and violence written on the page.

Hard Boiled novels, on the other hand, boast sex and violence. Historically, these novels featured hard-hitting detectives like Sam Spade and Philip Marlowe, but contemporary hard-boiled novels often star petty criminals and other mild deviants. The protagonists are tough, cool and unapologetic. They aren't afraid to shoot a man at close range or take a woman to bed on the first date, and Hard-Boiled authors will make sure all the gory details make it to the page.

While these two qualifiers are at opposite ends of the spectrum and many novels will fall somewhere in between, it is important to identify which subgenre your novel is closest to. Ask yourself the following:

> Is your protagonist an amateur sleuth or professional crime solver? Do they remind you of Marlowe and Spade or of Ms. Marpole and Lord Peter Wimsey?

Does your book have sex scenes? Is the door open or closed?

Do people die in your book? Does it happen on or off the page?

Are there curse words?

Could you read your novel to your church-going grandmother without blushing or offending her?

## Police Procedurals and Detective Fiction

On the cozy/hard-boiled spectrum, police procedurals and detective fiction generally fall somewhere in the middle. These novels feature a cop, detective, or P.I. as the main character and are often part of a series. In police procedurals, heavy emphasis is put on the "how" of solving a crime: crime scene investigation, canvassing, stakeouts, and other common procedures used by cops to solve crimes. Detective fiction is similar, but usually focuses more on the "why" rather than the "how". In detective fiction, the protagonist is usually haunted and the case strikes a personal chord. The readers care equally about the crime and the detective working to solve it.

Does your protagonist work in law enforcement?

Are forensics, ballistics, and other crime solving tools used in your novel?

Is your plot like a puzzle? Does the climax occur when all the pieces are in place?

If you answered yes to these questions, then your novel fits into the police procedure/detective fiction subgenre.

## Noir Fiction

Noir is a subgenre of Hard-Boiled fiction where the main character is someone directly involved with the crime, rather than a detective or P.I. who is summoned from the outside. In Noir Fiction, the victim or suspect is often the protagonist, giving readers a different vantage point than that of a standard mystery. The dark tone and use of sex and violence to further the plot is another attribute of noir fiction, one that sets it apart from police procedurals and other mysteries.

> Is your main character a victim or perpetrator of a crime?
>
> Is your main character seriously flawed?
>
> Do sex and violence play a large role in your story?

If you answered yes to these questions then you can call your novel Noir.

## Thriller Subgenres

Classifying thrillers is different than classifying mysteries. Thrillers are mostly differentiated by the theme of the story and occupation of the protagonist. But you have to be careful; just because your main character is a lawyer doesn't mean you've written a legal thriller. Ask yourself the following:

> What is your protagonist's occupation? Does their occupation play a central role in the novel? If you changed the protagonist's occupation, would the novel change at all?

Does your thriller address a specific theme or subject matter?

A few examples of thriller subgenre:

Legal thriller
Medical Thriller
Espionage Thriller
Action Adventure Thriller

The benefit of publishing a thriller with a clear subgenre is the same as mysteries: you immediately tap into an audience of readers. You can easily market your legal thriller to John Grisham readers or medical thriller to fans of Michael Crichton. You can easily hand your espionage thriller to a James Bond fanatic and say, "Read this, you'll like it." With the subgenre label displayed on the front cover, readers will know what to expect from your novel even if they have never heard of you. Agents and editors will have a clear idea of how to market the book and booksellers will know where to shelve you.

## Suspense Novels

If you are still unsure of whether or not your novel is a mystery or a thriller, a safe label to place across your manuscript is suspense. No matter what type of crime fiction you're writing, there should at least be suspense running throughout.

But of course, even suspense novels have their own subgenres:

### Romantic Suspense

By combining two of the most popular genres, romantic suspense authors are able to cross-pollinate audiences and reach a broad scope of readers. Typical romance novels include the blooming love between two people, but there are obstacles they must overcome to reach the necessary happy ending. In romantic suspense, those obstacles usually involve a crime or danger that is equally essential to the overall plot.

### Paranormal Suspense

Similar to Romantic Suspense, Paranormal Suspense combines two genres: crime fiction which has established its popularity and paranormal, which in recent years has exponentially increased in popularity. Paranormal indicates that there is an element of dark fantasy in the novel, whether it be werewolves, vampires, or psychics. Suspense indicates that the overall plot is still being driven by a crime or threatening circumstances, which is enhanced by the book's paranormal elements.

### Psychological Suspense

This particular label has a tendency to be misused by authors. Many authors deem their novels "Psychological Suspense" when they can't find another subgenre. After all, aren't all crimes psychological?

Brian Freeman, author of the Jonathan Stride series, describes a psychological suspense novel as one where, "The focus is really on why a crime took place to begin with. What was it about the backgrounds of the characters that drew them across a terrible line?" The plot isn't driven by uncovering a mystery or saving the world from mass destruction, and the story isn't centered around one character. Psychological suspense novels usually include many characters and explore why a crime took place or is taking place.

To use this label appropriately, ask yourself the following:

What is keeping the reader reading? Do they want to figure out the puzzle or understand the characters?

How many points of view are in your novel? Do you stick with the protagonist or hop into other characters' heads?

Though you may hate to put a label on your novel or slot it into some pre-determined category, identifying your book's genre and subgenre is a necessary step in the marketing process. These labels assist agents, editors, and eventually booksellers with marketing and selling your book. The list of subgenres can go on forever, and new ones are forming every day. Your novel may fall into one or two or five of the categories listed above. But by carefully analyzing your manuscript and asking yourself the preceding questions, you can accurately identify what type of novel you wrote and the best way to market it.

**Summary**

**Mystery Subgenres**
Cozy
Hard-boiled
Police Procedural/
Detective Fiction
Noir

**Thriller Subgenres**
Legal Thriller
Medical Thriller
Espionage Thriller
Action Adventure

**Suspense Subgenres**
Romantic Suspense
Paranormal Suspense
Psychological Suspense

# Scene of the Crime

# Setting
## by William Kent Krueger

In many books in the genre, the most important character has no flesh, no bone, no blood, and no voice, at least in the way we usually think of voice. Yet it's a character that can be loved or hated, that can strike fear in a heart or warm a heart, that has energy and personality and quirks and whims. And it always has a face as unique as any human's. I'm speaking, of course, about setting.

The word setting gets thrown around a lot and its meaning may be different for different writers and readers. So let's get straight what it is I'm talking about when I use the word.

What is setting?

**Setting is place.**

Globally speaking, setting is the environment in which the entire story occurs. LeHane's Dorchester, Burke's New Iberia, Sharyn McCrumb's Appalachia, Krueger's northern Minnesota. Speaking at another level, setting is the place where specific scenes occur within the story: An office, a park, a kitchen, a beach. And speaking at the most basic level, setting is what grounds the reader physically in every exchange or action that occurs in the story – reaching for the ketchup in the middle of the table, the sound of cars passing in the street, the smell of fry oil in a diner. So first and foremost setting is place.

**Setting is character.**

Like every human character, settings have physical characteristics that are unique and distinctive. A city vs. a small town. A neighborhood in New York vs. a neighborhood in L.A. The rural landscape of Mississippi as opposed to that of Minnesota. All as different as every one of you is from the others in this room. And all have distinct details that the eye of a reader ought to be able to see. Blonde, brunette, tall, short. What's the foliage like? What's the weather like? What are the houses like? How carefully maintained is the landscape? Women sometimes wear cologne and men sometimes smell of pipe tobacco. In your setting, what's the smell in the air?

Settings have personality. The personality of Michael Connelly's L.A. is very different from the personality of James Lee Burke's New Orleans. One is fast and hip and concrete and glitz. The other is slow and dank and humid and gritty. There's a unique feel to each of them that rises out of location and out of history and out of purpose. Joan Hess's small town of Maggody, Arkansas is nothing like Miller's Kill, New York, the small town in Julia Spencer Fleming's series. And it's not just that they're physically miles apart. Their personalities are miles apart. These towns have different cultures. They have different values.

Settings have voice. Drop a reader blindfolded into Dennis Lehane's south Boston or into J.A. Jance's Cochise County, without even being able to see, the reader is going to know she's in a different place. She's going to hear different things. The people speak differently. The land itself speaks differently. What you hear in south Boston: Cars and cursing and sound of ships' horns and jackhammers. That's worlds apart from what you hear in the Arizona desert: wind or coyotes or the singular rattle of a pickup's undercarriage over rough road or click of tumbleweed across pavement. They're both voices and they both communicate to the reader what kind of character the setting is.

**Setting is atmosphere.**

Think of the staging of a play. The lighting can be glaring or it can create shadows. The backdrops can be distinct or fuzzy or surreal. There can be mist floating across the stage. There can be lightning and the sound of thunder and rain. And all of these manipulations help create atmosphere for the audience. A book works the same way. Think about the moodiness in the landscape of DuMaurier's *Rebecca*. Think about Carl Hiassen's Florida, how glaring and surreal. Think about the shadowy streets of Raymond Chandler's L.A. The settings are used to create the atmosphere for the story.

**Setting is motivation.**

The actions that take place in a story ought to rise naturally out of the place in which they occur, and place ought to have a part in the reason for the story. The snuff movie industry in Lawrence Block's *Welcome to the Slaughterhouse* exists in large measure because of the kind of complex place that New York is. The child abduction in Dennis Lehane's *Gone Baby Gone* takes place because of the neglect in working class Dorchester. You remember the scene at the end of *Chinatown*. The cop turns Jake away from the horrific scene of the brutal shooting and says to him, "Forget it, Jake. It's Chinatown." Setting used correctly ought to contribute to the "why" of the story.

**Don't Deliver a Long Litany of Detail**

For godsake don't give the reader a travelogue. Think of creating your setting as you would create any character. You don't, generally speaking, spend long paragraphs introducing and describing a character, do you? You take your time and spread the salient details over time and you gradually reveal fully the nature of the character. It's more satisfying to the reader for so many reasons.

When creating setting think of the essence of place, and choose the details that will be both concrete and also suggestive of more. What do I mean by this? Here's an example:

> I'm not going to start off bitching and whining about how nothing ever happens in Maggody, for two reasons. One is that the promise is getting as stale as day-old bread. The other is that it doesn't appear to be all that valid anymore. That's not to say a lot of what happens in Maggody, Arkansas, isn't on the mundane side. We're talking about outsiders running the single traffic light or putting the pedal to the metal in the school zone. Dogs being stolen. Good ol' boys brawling at the pool hall on a regular basis. Marijuana and moonshine. Among Maggody's 755 residents, someone's always stirring up minor headaches for your truly, Alry Hanks, chief of police extraordinaire. I've got a real live badge and a box of three bullets to prove it.
>
> *Much Ado in Maggody,* Joan Hess

In a paragraph, Hess has given you a very few specific details and yet by the end of those few sentences you already have a pretty good handle on Maggody. You've taken what she's given you on the page and in your mind already begun to create a pretty fair image of the place.

In the same way you think of creating character, think of creating place. Think, of course, about the physical description, but be succinct as Raymond Chandler does in this example:

> It was one of those clear, bright summer mornings we get in the early spring in California before the high fog sets in. The rains are over. The hills are green and in the valley across the Hollywood hills you can see snow on the high mountains. The fur stores are advertising their annual sales. The call houses that specialize in sixteen-year-old virgins are

doing a land-office business. And in Beverly Hills the jacaranda trees are beginning to bloom.

*The Little Sister*, Raymond Chandler

Think about the personality. How do you suggest the culture of the place, the history, the voice?

Bone Street was local history. A crooked spine down the center of Watt's jazz heyday, it was four long and jagged blocks. West of Central Avenue and north of 103$^{rd}$ Street, Bone Street was broken and desolate to look at by day with its two-story tenement-like apartment buildings and its mangy hotels. But by night Bones, as it was called, was a center for late-night blues, and whiskey so strong that it could grow hairs on the glass it was served in. When a man said he was going to get down to the bare Bones he meant he was going to lose himself in the music and the booze and the women down there.

*White Butterfly*, Walter Mosley

Think about the psychological characteristics. How do you suggest a place full of menace? Or a place of repose? One way is the character's response to setting, as below:

The downtown library was on Flower and Figueroa. It was one of the oldest buildings in the whole city. Therefore it was dwarfed by the modern glass-and-steel structures that surrounded it. Inside it was a beauty, centered around a domed rotunda with 360-degree mosaics depicting the founding of the city by the *padres*. The place been twice burned by arsonists and closed for years, then restored to its original beauty. I had come after the restoration was completed, the first time back since I was a child. And I continued to come. It brought me close to the Los Angeles I remembered. Where I felt comfortable. I would take my lunch in the book rooms or the upper-level patios while reading case files and writing notes. I got to know the security guards and a few of the librarians. I had a library card, though I rarely checked out a book.

*Lost Light,* Michael Connelly

Don't say what you don't have to, but when you have to, sprinkle the details across the pages. Deliver place carefully and specifically. Don't interrupt the pace of the story.

As much as possible use the sections that deal with place to greater advantage than just the physical plane. Incorporate atmosphere or suspense or a broader sense of story:

> At the end of the continent, near the foot of Wilshire Boulevard, Jesse Stone stood and leaned on the railing in the darkness above the Santa Monica beach and stared at nothing, while below him the black ocean rolled away toward Japan.
>
> *Night Passage*, Robert B. Parker

## Entering A Story

Delivering a sense of place is a classic way of entering a story. It's just like introducing a new and intriguing character. Or in a series, reintroducing an old friend. It can incorporate any aspect of the character of the place you feel is important: the physical, the psychological, the emotional, the cultural, the historical. And if you can begin, especially, using the setting in relationship to the story or to an important character, that's always best. Stories are about relationship, so begin with relationship:

> January, as usual, was meat locker cold, and the girl had already been missing nearly two days. Corcoran O'Connor couldn't ignore the first circumstance. The second he tried not to think about.
>
> He stood in snow up to his ass, more than two feet of drifted powder blinding white in the afternoon sun. He

lifted his tinted goggles and glanced at the sky, a blue ceiling held up by green walls of pine. He stood on a ridge that overlooked a small oval of ice called Needle Lake, five miles from the nearest maintained road. Aside from the track his snowmobile had pressed into the powder, there was no sign of human life. A rugged vista lay before him – an uplifted ridge, a jagged shoreline, a bare granite pinnacle that jutted from the ice and that gave the lake its name – but the recent snowfall had softened the look of the land. In his time, Cork had seen nearly fifty winters come and go. Sometimes the snow fell softly, sometimes it came in a rage. Always it changed the face of whatever it touched. Cork couldn't help thinking that in this respect, snow was a little like death. Except that death, when it changed a thing, changed it forever.

*Blood Hollow,* William Kent Krueger

## Leaving A Story

Leaving a reader with a profound emotion is always a plus, and that emotion can often come from a final elucidation of the relationship between place and character. A final grounding, in the same way that a movie camera might sweep across a landscape while the background music swells:

> Neither sleep nor late-night thunderstorms bring them back now, and I rise each day into the sunlight that breaks through the pecan trees in my front yard. But sometimes at dusk, when the farmers burn the sugarcane stubble off their fields and cinders and smoke lift in the wind and settle on the bayou, when red leaves float in piles past my dock and the air is cold and bittersweet with the smell of burnt sugar, I think of Indians and water people, of voices that can speak through the rain and tease us into yesterday, and in that moment I scoop Alafair up on my shoulders and we gallop down the road through the oaks like horse and rider toward my house, where Batist is barbecuing *gaspagoo* on the

gallery and paper jack-o-lanterns are taped to the lighted windows, and the dragons become as stuffed toys, abandoned and ignored, like the shadows of the heart that one fine morning have gone with the season.

*Black Cherry Blues,* James Lee Burke

## Grounding The Reader

In every scene, the reader needs to be grounded. The reader needs to know the landscape in order to fully imagine the scene. So bring the thinking down from the global to the immediate. This is where the essence becomes really essential. Don't spend paragraphs describing a diner. Hell, everyone knows what a diner is. Give them one or two specific and telling details and let their imaginations do the rest, as in this classic example:

The pebbled glass door panel is lettered in flaked black paint: *"Phillip Marlowe....Investigations."* It is a reasonably shabby door at the end of a reasonably shabby corridor in the sort of building that was new about the year the all-tile bathroom became the basis for civilization.

*The Little Sister,* Raymond Chandler

Also, continue to ground the reader as the scene plays out. Don't let the action and dialogue take place in a vacuum. If your characters are in a diner, remind us. Dishes rattle or the juke box plays or the waitress calls out an order to the cook or your character reaches for a bottle to put ketchup on her hamburger.

## Augmenting Pace

Directing the reader's attention to the setting should never interrupt the flow or pace of the story. In fact, it ought to feed into the flow and help the pacing. This is where the judicious sprinkling of details of place comes into play. It can be especially useful for breaking up long sections of dialogue.

## Suggesting Emotion and Mood

Setting can be used to mirror a character's emotion or mood. Fog, rain, sun, wind can suggest a great deal more than just the weather. An empty street or a dark alley or silent house can be more than just the space through which your character moves physically. It can suggest the emotional landscape as well:

> I went back to the bench. The broad leaves of a dusty tree shaded me. Lizards flicked across the fitted stones of the pathways. A strolling dog eyed me in unfriendly inquiry. Two small boys wanted to shine my shoes. Two black and white goats stopped and snuffled among windblown debris. A fat brown man with one milky eye came smiling over and, with fragmentary English, tried to sell me a fire opal, then an elaborately worked silver crucifix, then a hand tooled wallet, then a small obscene wood carving, and then, in a coarse whisper, a date with a "friendly womans, nice and fat." He sighed and plodded away. I had the feeling I was the object of intense scrutiny, of dozens of people wondering how best to pry some of the Yankee dollars out of my pocket. I knew it would not have been that way before the hotel was built. But now the village had begun the slow transformation to the eventual mercilessness of Taxco, Cuernavaca, Acapulco. Too many Americans had shown them how easy it could be. Greed was replacing their inborn courtesy, pesos corrupting their morals. The village cop, agleam with whistles, bullets and buckles, strolled by, whapping himself on the calf with a riding crop.
> Nora was gone a long time. A very long time. Though I was watching the church, I did not see her until she was about twenty feet from me. Her color looked bad, her mouth pinched.
> "Let's walk," she said.
> I got up and went with her. "Bad?"

"He's a good man. It got to me a little. Let me just...unwind a little bit." She gave me a wry glance. "Mother Church. You think you've torn loose but...I don't know. I lit candles for him, Trav. I prayed for his soul. What would he think of that?"

"Probably he would like it."

We headed back out of town, toward La Casa Encantada. After we passed the last of the houses, there was a path worn through grass down toward the beach. She hesitated, and I nodded, and we went down the path. The beach was the village dump, cans and broken bottles and unidentifiable metal parts of things. There was some coarse brown-black sand, and outcroppings of shale, and tumbles of old seaworn rock. We went down where the tide kept it clean and after a hundred yards or so, came to an old piece of grey timber. She sat there and leaned on her knees and looked out. The big protective islands looked to be about eight miles offshore. An old fish boat was beating toward the town, with a lug-rigged sail tan as a lizard hide.

"He didn't speak very much, English, Trav. Enough I guess...."

*A Deadly Shade of Gold,* John D. MacDonald

## Creating Suspense

In the genre, this is a classic use of setting. In my novels characters often find themselves isolated in a forest, with every shadow suggesting menace. In a city, there are the dark corridors of the alleyways or the fog that obscures the street. There's the empty house with the sounds that suggest it's not so empty. And on and on. It's difficult to imagine creating suspense without using the setting.

To summarize, setting is the most versatile character in the story and used in more ways than any other character. A story without a solid sense of place is a ship lost in a great anonymous sea.

## Vics, Villains, and White Hats

# Captivating Characters
## by Jeanne Dams

I am sometimes asked what kind of books I like to read. That's not an easy question to answer, because I am an omnivorous reader. Classic fiction, new fiction, history, biography, philosophy, psychology, theology, children's books…really, it's easier to say what kind of books I dislike. But those I like have certain things in common. They're well-written; I will no longer tolerate a book whose author doesn't know, or doesn't respect, the basics of English grammar and syntax, or a book that insults my intelligence. The non-fiction books I enjoy either teach me something I didn't know, or present in a new light something I did know. As for fictional works, they are set in a place (real or imagined) that I want to visit, with characters I want to meet.

Perhaps it is obvious that the mystery is my favorite fictional genre, and some readers may be puzzled that I have not listed plot as one of my basic criteria for a "good" book. Certainly I want a good story. I want the author to spin a plot I can't figure out till the very end, and then I want to say, "Of course! I should have seen that all the time!" But a good plot is not my *first* requirement. I'll tolerate a trite plot, even an extremely unlikely dénouement, if the setting and the characters are sufficiently captivating.

When the mystery first developed as a popular genre, the plot was the driving force of the book or short story. Readers wanted a good puzzle to solve, wanted to match wits against the author. Setting tended to be unimportant; many of the early mysteries could have been set almost anywhere without changing the story much. Character was often overlooked, as well. Instead of flesh-and-blood human beings, too many authors gave us caricatures, stick figures like the Great Detective and the Idiot Sidekick; the Helpless Ingenue and the Master Criminal. Not that anyone minded much. The genre was new, it was lively, and the reading public ate it up.

Those days, I hope and trust, are gone forever. An increasingly sophisticated audience wants it all. Books and even short stories are character-driven rather than plot-driven. That is, the story grows out of realistic characters and their relationships, instead of the characters being invented to suit the needs of the story. A writer can no longer craft a book with a paint-by-number approach, drawing a plot outline and then filling in with a splotch of bright-blue Detective here and blood-red Villain there. Characters must be realistic. They must leave the page and enter the reader's heart and mind. They must make him, or her, cry or swear or sigh. They must keep him or her awake until three in the morning, unable to close the book until the characters' fates are resolved.

Memorize this: IF A READER DOESN'T CARE ABOUT THE CHARACTERS, HE WON'T FINISH THE BOOK. Note that I said "care about." The reader doesn't have to *like* all the characters. There will certainly be some characters the reader loves to hate. The point is that all the major characters, at least, must be so well-drawn that the reader knows them and responds to them, whether with affection or loathing, respect or distrust, sympathy or fear.

All right. How do you, the writer, create characters like that, characters that will make your reader want more, and more, and more from your fertile brain and ready computer? What's the secret? Where do you find these fascinating people? Do you go to CHARACTERS R US down the street and stock up?

Actually, I believe there really is a secret, and it's just this: you have to take your courage in both hands and put yourself into the book.

I can hear your groans even as I write this. You're raising your eyes to heaven and saying "Not more of that tired old 'write what you know' crap!" Well, yes, but not in quite the way you may think I mean it. Nor am I suggesting that you make your book autobiographical; most new writers tend to do that anyway.

Look at it this way: You've lived a life, for at least a few adult years and possibly a good many. You've had experiences, some wonderful, some awful, that have molded you. There is no one in the world who is like you; you are unique. You know things about your world, and about the people around you, from a perspective that is yours alone. You know about pain, and about bliss. What you must do now is tap into that experience and share it with your characters, who will pass it along to your readers.

I am not suggesting that this is easy. It can in fact be excruciating. Let me quote from one of my favorite authors, Dorothy L. Sayers. Her characters Harriet Vane and Lord Peter Wimsey are conversing. Harriet is a writer who incidentally has been tried for murder (and acquitted). She is stuck in the middle of a book, and has sought advice. Lord Peter speaks:

> "Couldn't you make Wilfrid one of those morbidly conscientious people, who have been brought up to think that anything pleasant must be wrong...? Give him a puritanical father and a hell-fire religion.... He'd still be a goop, and a pathological goop, but he'd be a bit more consistent.... You would have to abandon the jig-saw kind of story and write a book about human beings for a change."
>
> Harriet replies:
>
> "I'm afraid to try that, Peter. It might go too near the bone."
>
> "It might be the wisest thing you could do."
>
> "Write it out and get rid of it?"
>
> "Yes."
>
> "I'll think about that. It would hurt like hell."
>
> "What would that matter, if it made a good book?"
>
> *Gaudy Night,* Dorothy L. Sayers, 1935

Harriet doesn't want to reach into the recesses of her mind, where she has tried to bury painful memories. Peter is suggesting not only that "writing it out" will be good for Harriet psychologically, but that her experiences will enliven her characters and improve her book.

We who are writers have only ourselves to put into our books. I can't remember who said that to write one had only to sit down and open a vein, but it's absolutely true. We write about people: their failures and successes, their aspirations and disappointments, their actions and reactions. We have met many people in the course of our lives, but there is only one person whom we know intimately, right down to the nastiest habits and ugliest thoughts and silliest daydreams. If we are to create a hero, we don't just read about David or Gandhi or Martin Luther King or Harry Potter. Yes, we do all that, but then we search our own psyche to find whatever heroic qualities we possess. We imagine what it's like to confront Goliath or colonial oppressors or racists or evil wizards. We remember that time we were so scared of the school bully we almost wet our pants, but we somehow managed not to back down.

And then...and then...we go to the next page and find we must get into the mind of the villain. That's even more painful. None of us likes to admit, even to ourselves, that we have an intimate understanding of evil, but it's there. Remember the time that guy cut you off on the Interstate and you almost ended up in the ditch? Remember the rage that boiled up, the things you thought, or screamed? Remember when that aunt you didn't like anyway punished you for what your cousin did, that he lied about? You were eight, and for a moment at least you could have killed both of them for the injustice of it all.

When I was writing full time, I used to come up from my basement office so tired I could barely drag myself up the stairs, and I would wonder what had worn me out so. I came to realize that I had lived through every emotion my characters had experienced that day. I had in very fact *been* the murderer, terrified he would be discovered, and the grieving mother of the victim, and the detective grimly pursuing justice, and even the gossipy neighbor talk-talk-talking to keep fear at bay. No wonder I was exhausted!

I have often said that the author of fiction can't hide. You reveal yourself on every page – your convictions, your fears, your world-view. Or if you don't, you should. You can shove your real self firmly to the back of your mind and write a slick, glib piece of nonsense, or you can open a vein and write a masterpiece.

Enough theory; let's get to technique. You want practical suggestions about how to achieve your goal. Your characters will probably begin by resembling someone you know. All mine do, anyway. I find it impossible to imagine a person who is totally unlike any of my friends, relations, or enemies. But of course your characters can't remain like the real people on whom they're based – for two reasons. The obvious one is that you risk an action for libel if a character is recognizable as a real person. The other, and more important, reason is what I call "the tyranny of the real." You will find yourself thinking, as you write about the heroine based on your friend Jane, "Oh, but Jane wouldn't do that." You're probably quite right, but the thought is irrelevant. You must divorce yourself from the thought of the real Jane and concentrate on what your character Sarah will do in the situation. She might react more like your Aunt Betty, or your neighbor Nancy, or…. The point is that the character must become herself, even if she has begun as Jane.

That means that you must know Sarah, and all your principal characters, thoroughly. And the best way to accomplish that is to develop a biography of each of them. It may include, among other things, their:

1. level of education

2. occupation
3. temperament
4. lifestyle
5. marital status and sexual orientation
6. kids?
7. background (parents, etc.)
8. politics
9. religion
10. favorite things
11. appearance

Note that I've put appearance last. That's because it is generally the least important. Your reader will make up his own mental image of the character from the other information you supply, if you do it skillfully. A few pertinent details will suffice – the mustache, the white hair, the acne. The exception to this rule is the fairly rare instance in which a character's appearance is a major plot point. If you're writing about Cyrano de Bergerac or Helen of Troy you can scarcely leave out the long nose or the incredible beauty.

These biographies are boring, slogging work. You want to get on with writing your book. But the book will go much better once you really know your characters. Trust me.

Once you get into the swing of your book, and your characters begin to come alive, they will often tell you that you were wrong about parts of their biographies. One of them isn't at all the self-confident braggart that he seems; under that façade he's painfully shy. The one you thought was the murderer turns out to be the kind of person who can't kill so much as a spider. Within reason, and the limitations of your plot, let your characters develop as they will. Beware, though, of the charming, handsome man who turns out to be the double-dyed villain, or the prostitute with the heart of gold. They were originally brilliant fictional devices, but they have become clichés of the very worst kind. Me, I've learned never, ever to trust a charming guy encountered early in a book – which means the smart author can make him the real hero of the piece, having fooled me completely.

Well, but just how do you get your characters to the point that they live and breathe on their own? How do you get the reader to know them as well as you do?

That's an easy one. How do you know real people, your friends, family, neighbors? Notice I said *know*, not *recognize*. You *recognize* them by their appearance, but you *know* them by their words and actions. Very well. As a writer you don't have pictures as part of your tool kit, but you have words, and words can describe actions. Let your characters speak and act "in character," and *voilà*! They walk right off the page.

So here we come to that other piece of instruction you've come to know and hate: show, don't tell. Sorry, but it's a vital piece of advice. Never tell us a character is shy. Show her hesitating before walking into a room full of strangers. She looks around, then wipes her damp hands on her skirt before sitting on the chair closest to the door. She never opens her mouth until someone speaks to her, and then says, "No. I mean yes. I don't know," and looks away.

Which brings us to the most useful tool you have for delineating character: dialogue. Dialogue is at the very heart of well-written fiction. It can do so many things at once: reveal character, advance plot, create atmosphere. Indeed, it must do all these things. There is no room, even in the 75,000 or so words of a novel, for empty dialogue.

Here is another instance where the tyranny of the real can intrude. You must not write "real" dialogue. Real dialogue – the way real people really talk – is often deathly boring. Eavesdrop some time on the couple at the next table, or in the grocery store. If you hear anything scintillating, or even moderately interesting, I'll give you ten bucks next time I see you. You can't write dialogue like that. Yours must impart some information to the reader. Note the inane little speech I created a couple of paragraphs ago. Boring? Of course. But it's boring on purpose, to help the reader get to know this poor girl.

Here's an exercise for you. Create a dialogue between a youngish guy who just got out of prison and a sweet, white-haired grandmother. He's white; she's African-American. Let only the dialogue tell us these details, using the way they speak to delineate their personalities – in other words, to create their characters.

You will have to develop your own techniques for making your characters speak and behave realistically. The one I have found most useful is to act them out. I sit at my computer and become the character, in the situation. If the character is supposed to be jubilant, I smile, perhaps bounce out of my chair, dance around the room a bit – whatever feels right for this character in this situation. Then I sit back down and write the character doing what I just did, and saying what came to my mind as I acted out his, or her, emotions. It's fun when the character is happy, not much fun when the character is depressed or terrified. For me it works. Try it. If it's not useful for you, try other techniques until you find one that enables you to get right into the skin of your characters.

Finally, when you have finished a scene, read it aloud, preferably to a discerning friend. If it sounds real, if you and your friend can see these people, feel what they're feeling – you've succeeded. If not, go back and rewrite, or study the biographies to see where you've gone wrong, or rethink the characters – whatever it takes to make them come alive. And never forget that reader out there who is eagerly awaiting a new book with characters who spring off the page. Good luck!

# Choosing the Right Point of View
## by Mary Saums

For weeks now, you've considered and re-considered your idea for a mystery novel. You can't seem to think of anything else. You enjoy imagining your main character's current situation and his past. You anticipate the hardships you'll throw at him with glee. The setting is one you know well and love. The victim will have a strong resemblance to your ex-boss. The plot twist at the end is a killer.

You can't wait to fire up your laptop and begin putting your dreams into words on the screen. But before they can start flying out of your fingertips, you have an important decision to make. Who will tell your story? What point of view will work best for the story you want to tell?

The answer is, as with most things in life, it depends.

If you're starting your first novel, don't despair. Most writers want to write the kind of books they love to read. You've most likely tried different types of mysteries and have found a certain sub-genre you like to read best. Think of what you loved about a few of your favorites. Keep those things in mind as we take a look at the most common point of view choices in today's mysteries.

## First Person

In first person point of view, the main character tells the story using "I" as he relates all events from beginning to end. The reader knows only what the main character sees or experiences himself. This means he must be in every scene you write, relating everything that happens in the story. He cannot know what anyone else thinks or feels, only what they do or say.

Since the reader spends so much time inside the protagonist's head, first person naturally allows you more time to fully develop the protagonist's character. His reactions and feelings are on display. This tends to make the reader feel closer and more invested in him. For that reason, first person is a good choice for a series character, one readers will want to revisit.

Though first person limits reader information to only what the narrator knows, this isn't all bad in a mystery. When the detective is in the dark, this creates suspense for the reader who will, along with the detective, wonder what's going to happen next.

One good example of first person used in a traditional mystery novel comes from Donna Andrews:

> I had become so used to hysterical dawn phone calls that I only muttered one halfhearted oath before answering.
> "Peacocks," a voice said.
> "I beg your pardon, you must have the wrong number," I mumbled. I opened one eye to peer at the clock: it was 6:00 A.M.
>
> *Murder With Peacocks*, Donna Andrews

For a private eye novel:

> Damp, soupy heat washed over me as I pushed out through the revolving door. The bright morning glare was already hazed up by the shimmering exhaust of a river of cars, buses, and trucks. I looked left, looked right, got my bearings, and headed briskly down the sidewalk.
> "Come on!" I turned to yell to my partner, Bill Smith, who still stood, looking a little groggy, his hands in his pockets, just gazing around. "Relive your misspent youth some other time! I don't want to be late."
>
> *Reflecting the Sky*, S. J. Rozan

Or a police procedural:

> "Where's the chief?" Ceepak asks Gus at the front desk.
> "Down at the boardwalk for the big show."

"We have a situation."

The way Ceepak says "situation," I know we're in trouble. Big time.

*Mad House*, Chris Grabenstein

And noir:

Then there's the zoning, from the time I was a child, I'd go someplace in my mind, a cold place and it's like seeing the world through a fog or very heavy glass and what I most want is to do damage, biblical damage, it's beyond rage, more like a controlled fury that oh so careful watches, then strikes. I saw a cobra once on the TV and that hooded head, the poise and then the ferocious strike . . .

*Once Were Cops*, Ken Bruen

Please note how POV plus the sub-genre helps to create voice.

## Third Person

With third person, the narrator tells the story using "He" or "She." Third can be used either with one viewpoint character throughout the book, as in first person above, or with multiple viewpoints in the course of the story.

Multiple viewpoints can give a broader feel to the story since scenes aren't necessarily tied to a single narrating character. This method can also allow the reader to know more than the detective knows at times. For example, if one scene shows a villain putting a bomb in a box, and a later scene shows the detective receiving a parcel, you've provided good suspense and put your readers a little ahead of the game. Multiple viewpoints work well in stories of international intrigue that focus more on action and plot rather than character development.

In *Still Life*, a traditional mystery, Louise Penny uses multiple third person POVs. Following are short excerpts from Gamache's POV and then Clara's:

> Chief Inspector Armand Gamache of the Sûreté du Quebec knelt down; his knees cracking like the report of a hunter's rifle, his large, expressive hands hovering over the tiny circle of blood marring her fluffy cardigan, as though like a magician he could remove the wound and restore the woman. But he could not. That wasn't his gift. Fortunately for Gamache he had others. The scent of mothballs, his grandmother's perfume, met him halfway. Jane's gentle and kindly eyes stared as though surprised to see him.
>
> Clara's jaw dropped. Her head jerked down as though suddenly insupportable. Her eyes widened and her breathing stopped. It was as though she'd died, for an instant. So this was Fair Day. It took her breath away. And clearly the other jurors felt the same way. There were varying degrees of disbelief on the semi-circle of faces. Even the chairperson, Elise Jacob, was silent. She actually looked like she was having a stroke.
>
> Clara hated judging other people's work, and this was the worst so far.
>
> *Still Life*, Louise Penny

A police procedural could sound like this:

> Now he picked the letter out of the bin, replaced it in the envelope and put it in his jacket pocket. Later, he'd put it through the office shredder.
>
> A worse thought: some joker on his own team had done this as a hoax. They were waiting to see his reaction.
>
> Well, he wouldn't give them that satisfaction. Bugger it, he'd check their reactions. He got up and took his usual route between the desks towards the door at the far end, appearing nonchalant while alert to any suggestion of a snigger. At one point he stopped and swung round as if he'd forgotten a file and needed to go back.
>
> No one was paying him any attention.

Two, at least, had their eyes on Ingeborg, the novice detective, as she bent over a filing cabinet. Keith Halliwell, the longest-serving DI – and well capable of practical joking – was on the phone. The civilian staff were fingering their keyboards.

*The Secret Hangman*, Peter Lovesey

And noir:

"I guess I'm going home," Hop told the bartender at the King Cole, pushing the empty glass forward with his two index fingers. His head wobbled and he knew he'd had at least two drinks too many. *Fuck me, I'm innocent.*

"It's not even two. King Cole's booming until four o'clock closing."

"Maybe so." Hop threw some bills on the bar, his eyes moving in and out of focus. "But I got someone waiting."

"A girl?"

"Sort of. A wife."

It was only then that, in his bourbon haze, Hop remembered there was no wife. Hadn't been one for almost a month. The only place to see Midge now was tucked in Jerry's brown-walled bachelor pad on Bronson. It was the first time he'd forgotten and it made him feel lost, a ship knocking against a dock over and over that no one hears.

*The Song Is You*, Megan Abbott

Showing thoughts through the use of italics as above is a common way, although the phrase "he thought" can be used (drop italics if you do it this way) or simply he knew xyz.

## Limited and Omniscient

When writing in third person, you have a choice of a limited or omniscient viewpoint. With limited third, you write using "He" or "She" but with the same constraint used in first person, that is, the reader is only told what the viewpoint character is seeing or thinking. Or, if using multiple viewpoints as in the example from *Still Life*, what those characters experience and think.

In omniscient viewpoint, the reader can know anything from any character's viewpoint at any time – including the author's viewpoint. This is used frequently in literary novels but rarely in mysteries. Here's an example of omniscient point of view from a master. Listen for the authorial voice that is clearly heard:

[Charlie] Moon pushed his black Stetson back a notch to a jaunty position, looped an arm around the old woman's shoulders. "You should move into town."

Daisy snorted. "Why should I do a thing like that?"

"I worry about you." The tall man looked down at the top of her head. "In Ignacio, you'd have neighbors to look in on you."

"Neighbors – hah! I'd sooner have a family of skunks nesting under my floor." Her lips crinkled into an enigmatic smile. *And it's not like I'm all by myself . . . .*

The quiet in this remote place was more than the absence of sound. It was a peaceful river, flowing slowly out of the canyon. For a few heartbeats, it seemed as if Moon and Daisy were the only human beings in the world.

They were not, of course.

The planet was bustling and crackling with billions of busy people. All over the globe, on a multitude of stages, small and large dramas were being played out.

For example: About four hundred miles south of the Southern Ute reservation, something very big and bad and noisy was about to happen – an event that would, in time, unsettle the lives of Charlie Moon and his aunt Daisy.

*Shadow Man*, James D. Doss

## Mixing It Up?

Only a few years ago, mixing first and third person viewpoints within a mystery was not the thing to do. Today, some authors have been successful in doing this. Frequently, serial killer novels and other thrillers have prologues written in third person from the viewpoint of the villain, with the body of the novel written in first person in the good guy's viewpoint.

Other authors alternate first and third person sections without the use of prologues. Joan Hess does so in her comic Maggody mystery series. Harlan Coben also does this very well in his standalone thriller, *Tell No One*.

I'd advise sticking with one or the other point of view for new writers. However, one tried and true way to mix it up just a little bit without confusing your readers is by using diaries or letters written in first person, with the rest of novel written in third person. Readers are accustomed to this, so as long as the section is set apart or in italics, they won't be scratching their heads and wondering what's going on.

Don't be afraid to experiment with different points of view to find the right one for your book. Read widely to learn how the pros use viewpoint to enhance their readers' enjoyment. That's the bottom line, to present a great experience to your readers. And if you happen to have fun along the way, so much the better. Good luck!

# Tick, tick, tick . . .

# Building Suspense
## by Libby Fischer Hellmann

The President of the United States is held hostage. Jack Bauer is prosecuted for torture. A nuclear bomb is set to explode over Los Angeles. If you've ever watched "24," you're familiar with these scenarios. If you haven't, I recommend watching a season or two. The plot machinations can be over the top, and some of the dialogue is so lame it's dead-to-rights funny. But nowhere else will you see so many edge-of-your-seat stories presented and drawn out, sometimes over the course of an entire season.

What "24" has done relentlessly – and well – is build suspense. Whether it's a global crisis, or an individual melt-down, suspense is not so much what *is* happening, as what *may* happen. It's about anticipation, often anticipating the worst. It's about creating an uncertain situation in which the outcome is in doubt. It's asking a question not immediately answered, raising a concern not immediately addressed, posing a threat not immediately resolved.

Notice that *immediately* is the key word. Suspense depends on stretching out time – delaying answers as long as possible. The longer the writer can stretch and delay, the longer information is parceled out in bits, the more suspense there is.

Before I became a writer, I read John Le Carre, Robert Ludlum, Ken Follett, Len Deighton, Frederick Forsyth and others (the suspense genre, with the exception of romantic suspense, was dominated by males back then). I loved the nail-biting scenes, the emotional roller-coasters, the utter inability to put the book down. I knew before I wrote my first novel that suspense would be an integral part of my craft.

But suspense is not limited to crime fiction. Any story with a secret, tension, or unresolved conflict is ripe for the kind of unbearable, exquisite suspense so many of us love.

Consider some of the greatest classics in English literature: *To Kill A Mockingbird*; *Moby Dick*; *Wuthering Heights*, *The Great Gatsby*. All of them use suspense to heighten interest and emotion. Contemporary authors as well, including Jodi Picoult, Margaret Atwood, and many more, incorporate suspense in their novels.

Thus, I believe suspense should be a critical element in every author's tool-kit. To that end, following are some techniques, culled from master story-tellers and authors you may know, to build suspense in your work.

## The Hook

A first line gives readers an indication of the novel's voice, character, sometimes setting. But that first sentence must also provoke, tease, or set up a situation that compels the reader to *keep* reading. First lines need to have enough suspense to hook the reader at the outset. Consider the following:

> The man with ten minutes to live was laughing.
> *The Fist of God*, Frederick Forsyth

> The small boys came early to the hanging.
> *Pillars Of The Earth*, Ken Follett

> For a week, the feeling had been with him, and all week long young Paul LeBaeau had been afraid.
> *Iron Lake*, William Kent Krueger

> Ricki Feldman is best admired from a distance – if you get too close, you might find some of your body parts missing.
> *An Image of Death*, Libby Fischer Hellmann

I was trapped in a house with a lawyer, a bare-breasted woman, and a dead man. The rattlesnake in the paper sack only complicated matters.

*Fat Tuesday*, Earl Emerson

My bodyguard was mowing the yard wearing her pink bikini when the man fell from the sky.

*Dead Over Heels*, Charlaine Harris

I turned the Chrysler onto the Florida Turnpike with Rollo Kramer's headless body in the trunk, and all the time I'm thinking I should have put some plastic down.

*Gun Monkeys*, Victor Gischler

Each opening is unique, but they share something as well: each line begins in the middle of the action, *in medias res*. The reader knows something is already in progress, something they need to catch up on. Something intriguing or captivating. As you can see, first lines don't have to be serious. Humor can be suspenseful, too. Whether serious or funny, the challenge is to craft a first sentence so artfully that a reader MUST read on.

## The Sting

At the other end of a chapter is another opportunity to hook the reader. The goal here is to create a "sting" or cliff-hanger, a proven technique of suspense. Again, the objective is to leave the action in *in medias res* so that it's impossible for the reader to put the book down.

A variation of the sting is to introduce a totally new concept, danger, or character at the end of a chapter that must be followed up immediately. Either way, if it's done right, readers will be compelled to go on. In "24," for example, most scenes do end with a sting, but it works just as well in prose. Consider these:

"He was arrested a few weeks ago, and he's in jail. They say he killed a teenage girl."
*Easy Innocence*, Libby Fischer Hellmann

Pony tail plunged the needle into his chest. The old man's hands flew up. The dog biscuit fell and skittered across the floor.
*An Eye for Murder*, Libby Fischer Hellmann

Petrovsky started the Buick and pulled out of the lot. Davis backed out and swung the wheel left. The car went into a skid. "Fuck." She muttered under her breath.
I belted myself in.
*An Image of Death*, Libby Fisher Hellmann

As they pulled her to her feet, the cold metal of a gun barrel nuzzled her neck.
*An Image of Death*

A cautionary note: don't create a sting at the end of every chapter. If overused, the sting becomes redundant and trite. Readers need periods of calm between the storms.

### Raise the stakes

Perhaps you've heard an editor or reviewer say, "What's at stake?" or "The stakes aren't high enough." What they mean is that the reader doesn't have enough emotional investment in the story or character. An author must create that investment by continually raising the stakes: increasing the danger; ramping up the possibilities for disaster; and in doing so, escalating suspense at every turn. Happily, there are several techniques that will do that in your fiction.

### Create complications

Confront your protagonist with obstacles and dangers and stresses that must be managed or overcome. Sometimes those dangers might be hidden, and the character won't realize they're there. For example, a heroine starts to undress thinking she is alone and safe, but unbeknownst to her, the villains are climbing up the fire escape. The suspense comes from the reader wondering whether she'll hear them in time and be able to escape.

### Develop a Worst-Case Scenario

Another way to raise the stakes is to think of your worst case scenario... and then make it worse. For example, a protagonist might think he's killed the villain. At the last minute, though, the villain rises, draws a bead on the hero, and threatens him... again.

A fine example of a worst-case scenario occurs in William Kent Krueger's *Purgatory Ridge*. Two women and three children have been kidnapped. The women try to escape, pitting their lives and those of their children against the risk and dangers, not only of a crazy gunman but a harsh Minnesota winter. But even that's not enough. It turns out one of children is diabetic and needs insulin or he'll die. The stakes are suddenly sky high.

### Create dilemmas

Another way to raise the stakes is to tempt a character with no-win situations or Hobbesian choices. For example, a character can only save one person – another must die. A character picks up a gun after swearing an oath never to do so. A character is faced with alcohol after years of sobriety. Confronting a character with questions of morality creates tension and suspense. The reader knows the wrong choice will mean danger, risk, perhaps the loss of everything for which the character has worked.

## Isolate the protagonist

One of the best ways to establish close identification with readers, and thus, raise the stakes, is to make the protagonist face tests and obstacles alone. Through the course of the story, a protagonist should become increasingly isolated. His friends, colleagues, even his tools, are stripped away, forcing him to confront the enemy alone. Think of Ludlum's *Bourne Identity*: Jason Bourne, unsure whom he can trust, performs tasks by himself, using his wits to overcome danger. Sometimes, in the process, he develops new skills. Because readers identify with him, they root for him. They want him to succeed. The stakes and the suspense are high.

## Include the antagonist's POV

In many crime fiction novels, there's a chance the reader already knows – or suspects – the identity of the villain. Suspense builds when the writer explores the antagonist's point of view and gives readers reasons why this person is the way they are. Perhaps the writer even creates sympathy for the villain – at least understanding. Knowing the antagonist's character, motivation, and thoughts adds conflict by pitting two adversaries against each other. In that way, it also ratchets up the drama and suspense.

This can be done in small ways or large. Perhaps we're in the antagonist's thought process as the villain finishes a meal. Or perhaps the writer describes his thoughts as he confronts the protagonist in the climax. However it's done, the reader must believe in and fear this person. When readers see how calculating, manipulative or evil the villain is, or conversely, how misunderstood they are, they will react viserally. And when that happens, the author has raised the stakes.

## MacGuffins and Red Herrings: Structural Misdirection

Another way to build suspense is more structural. In a way, it's the natural evolution of differing POVs. It involves planting a character, clue, or event intended to mislead the protagonist and the reader. One of the best examples of structural misdirection I know was the ending of "The Sopranos." The scene was full of red herrings that added to the suspense: the daughter trying to park her car; the menacing man at the bar; the cut-aways to the bathroom; the shots of Carmella eating onion rings. What eventually happened? Take a look at the show, if you don't already know. That's structural misdirection.

The MacGuffin (named originally by Alfred Hitchcock) is a more complex version of the red herring, and its effect is more than simply raising the stakes. A writer using a MacGuffin actually creates subplots and characters that provide alternative scenarios for the murder or the crime. It's intended to distract and confuse. While the protagonist – as well as the reader – are focused on the MacGuffin, the antagonists are solidifying their hold on the real situation. Suspense builds when the MacGuffin is revealed. Because time has been wasted and energies depleted, the opportunity for the protagonist to prevail is that much more limited. The stakes are higher; the suspense tauter.

Hitchcock was a master of the MacGuffin. But it's been used by Agatha Christie, Dashiell Hammett (*The Maltese Falcon*), and even filmmaker Robert Altman in *Gosford Park*.

## Delay Revelations

Essentially the MacGuffin delays revelations. And delaying revelations is an excellent way to prolong suspense. When the moment of revelation is forestalled – when the protagonist is kept in ignorance as long as possible – a writer plays to universal fears. Moreover, once the door has been opened and the information revealed, the scare may fade. Think about the film *Signs* with Mel Gibson. During the first part of the film, the audience doesn't know what evil is confronting his family. Because of that, the film is riveting. Once we discover the threat are just aliens, it becomes anti-climatic. Just another "ho-hum" scifi film. In prose, there are several ways to forestall revelations.

## Shifting POVs, Time, Locations

Varying one or more of these elements can delay revelations, and thus build suspense. Perhaps the most classic example is the Hitchcockian example of the bomb under the table. If two people are playing cards, and the bomb goes off, you have surprise, even shock. However, when the camera cuts from the card players to the ticking bomb, back to the card players, then back to the bomb, the situation is gripping and emotional – and suspenseful.

You'll see shifting frequently in "24." Split screens typically bookend each scene, recapping not just Jack Bauer's perspective, but those of his team members, adversaries, and victims as well. Cutting back and forth between the characters and locations builds momentum, keeps interest from waning, and allows viewers to invest in the story.

## Teaser Resolution

Presenting an apparent resolution, quickly followed by an additional complication, can build suspense. The villain is not really dead... the task is not really completed... the danger has not really passed. I used this technique in *A Picture of Guilt*. Ellie Foreman's colleagues disarm a suitcase bomb and think all is well. Then they pick up traces of a second device, which, because of its location, could be even more threatening. The suspense is gripping.

## Stretch Time

The corollary of delaying revelations is to stretch time. The objective is to draw out time and extend it as much as possible, particularly during action sequences. In *A Picture of Guilt*, for example, my protagonist, Ellie, and an FBI agent are tracking a nuclear device, poised to detonate at any minute. I drew it out for four chapters. Following are some techniques to help stretch time.

## Literary Slow Motion

At peak moments of conflict, try to stretch the moment with sensory details. Let's say the hero has been beaten up and is lying on the floor. The writer might describe what he's seeing, hearing, and feeling, including:

- The villain's shoes coming at him
- The lights dimming
- His vision blurring
- The sound of rustling, or laughing, or shouting

Couple that with a stinger at the end of the scene, such as, "His last conscious thought was of – " and you have suspense. Author William Goldman used literary slow motion quite effectively in *Heat,* where he takes seven pages to describe eighteen seconds. When time is slowed down to that extent, the reader stays riveted.

## Deadlines

One of the most common techniques used to stretch time is to impose a deadline by which something must – or must not – happen. The protagonist is working against the clock, and the clock should be working for the antagonists, taking the protagonist farther away from his goal. In Robert Ludlum and Gayle Lynds' *The Altman Code,* covert agent Jon Smith has only days to prove the Chinese are sending chemical weapons to Iraq. In Greg Iles' *24 Hours,* Will and Karen Jennings have one day to escape their captor to rescue their child from a kidnapper. But many literary and cinematic works that *aren't* crime fiction use deadlines as well, for example, the films *An Affair to Remember* and *High Noon,* Shakespeare's comedy *Midsummer Night's Dream,* even Dickens' *Tale of Two Cities.*

## Count-downs

Breaking up time into smaller pieces can add even more suspense. In "24" the ticking clock is a staple. Each episode is one hour of a day, and each block of the show is book-ended with a digital clock. Whether in film or prose, the use of real-time, especially when it's being counted down, creates urgency and tension. The reader is aware a deadline is approaching and time is running out. In an example of a written "count-down" scene, the narrative might say, "Ten minutes were left…" at which point dialogue or action would occur. Then, "She looked at her watch. Five minutes remained." More action or dialogue. Then, "Two minutes to go." Something else happens.

The technique is not limited to time. *Distance* can also be used as a count-down. For example, "He was two hundred yards away. I reached into my pocket. At one hundred yards. I pulled out my gun. When he got within fifty yards..." and so on. *Setting* or *Location* can also be stretched. "In DC Mary did this ... In New York, John did this. In Paris, Jacque was doing this." When these elements are juxtaposed with a deadline, the suspense should be almost unbearable.

Finally, suspense, while critical to crime fiction, needs to be integrated with the other elements of fiction. Conflict, pacing, action, character development, dialogue, voice, language – a writer needs to juggle all these to master their craft.

# "Just Whistle"

# Dynamic Dialogue
## by Mark Zubro

Dialogue is the dynamic of a story. With it you are able to tell the readers directly and indirectly volumes about your character.

## Things I've Learned

(Fair warning – there are exceptions to every rule and dictum here below. And bending and breaking any of the rules and dictums – sure. These aren't written in stone although my high-speed, believes-itself-omnipotent, Mac computer thinks they are.)

I have found reading my dialogue out loud is stunningly helpful. If you happen to be in a reading group, reading your dialogue with them, I have found, is even more stunningly helpful. It helps get the sounds and the rhythms right. It helps make sure your characters are speaking in appropriate ways for who and what they are.

Yes, the old carry-a-notebook-with-you dictum is true. The notebook can be small and unnoticeable. Yes, I've written down snippets of dialogue on napkins, newspaper margins, whatever comes to hand. This isn't usually from eavesdropping. I can't remember, at this moment, getting any good dialogue from eavesdropping. As far as I can see that technique is highly over-rated. No, it's mostly things that sound perfect from people who I'm actually talking to and I write down. Sometimes, I just outright ask if I can use the phrase or comment someone has just said in a book. So far they've always said yes.

And speaking of eavesdropping – if you've got characters acting and reacting because of something they overheard, be very, very careful. It's a cliché. It's a lazy, easy way out for an author. Would someone believe a character who walked around listening at doors as a lifestyle?

Although, in actual fact, I knew someone who did that, but put it in fiction? Who's going to believe that? Like I said, be careful. You want a mystery, not soap opera.

Calling people by their name in dialogue is very annoying. Politicians and salesmen might do this, but unless you've got a crowd scene and are trying to identify who is talking to whom, it usually jars the reader's sensibility. Well, okay, it jars my sensibility. And we've recently seen this cliché acted out and mocked on the national stage.

Lose the adverbs. All of them. Period. Sorry about that, you adverb lovers.

Don't give someone's life story in dialogue. Just use exposition and be done with it. No one talks in lengthy compound complex paragraphs.

People talk in contractions. Yours should too.

Stick to plain old quotation marks. No editor is going to let a book get into print with a new way of punctuating dialogue. Well, okay, they might. You really want to take the chance yours is going to be the exception? And speaking of punctuation marks – rules of grammar don't have to apply to dialogue. Fragments, run-ons, incomplete sentences – knock your socks off and have a good time – just do it judiciously.

Stick to only the important stuff your characters say. Hello, how are you, I am fine, want some coffee, cream and sugar, and on and on. Trust me, no one cares. Unless what someone puts in the coffee is deadly poison and even then, do you really want to draw attention to it?

If your characters all sound alike, you've got it wrong. Sorry.

You've got to match your dialogue to your characters and to their actions. A thumb twiddling, horn-rimmed glasses wearing character reveals a certain thing to a reader. Now, you can sometimes have the thumb twidler, etc. talk in a deep bass voice and wear tight leather pants, but be careful. The contrast could be illuminating, but it is also likely to be distracting. Do it more than a few times, and it could be deadly.

If your character is performing actions, they can be revealing but avoid making it tedious. Mrs. Jones poured tea as if the queen of England were sitting next to her while she explained in gruesome detail her method if disemboweling corpses, is more likely better than Mrs. Jones picked up the cup, daintily held the saucer, gently and surely (oh, look, adverbs) poured the precise number of drops into the cup, lifted the sugar spoon, took two hundred forty-seven grains of sugar out of the bowl, brought it over the steaming liquid, and carefully deposited them into the cup while she explained in gruesome detail her method of disemboweling corpses. If it's a lengthy dialogue scene, sure the characters can shift around. Or you can add extraneous bits of author commentary. See the opening of *Hugger Mugger* by Robert Parker for a great example of information given through dialogue that also reveals character – his own and his clients'. A small bit from the opening of *Hugger Mugger*:

"I was at Claiborne Farms once and actually met Secretariat," I said. "He gave a large lap."

He smiled a pained smile. Horse people, I have noticed, are not inclined to think of horses in terms of how, or even if, they kiss.

"That's fine," he said.

Penny sat straight in her chair, her hands folded in her lap, her knees together, her ankles together, her feet firmly on the floor. She was wearing white gloves and a set of pearls, and a dark blue dress that didn't cover her knees. I was glad that it didn't.

"I own Three Fillies Stables. Named after my three daughters. We're in Lamarr, Georgia."

"Racehorses," I said.

"Yes, sir. I don't breed them, I buy and syndicate."

Penny was wearing shoes that matched her dress. They were conservative heels, but not unfashionable. Her ankles were great.

"In the past month," Clive said, "there has been a series of attacks on our horses."

"Attacks?"

We're getting information here mixed with description. Penny is a certain kind of rigid, and Parker is a certain kind of appreciative, all in the middle of giving and getting information essential to the plot.

Also, on performing actions – people often use gestures when they talk. See if there's something that your characters are saying that might be accompanied by a gesture. The old scratch of the head when trying to think type of thing, but, of course, not done in an old clichéd way. And avoid actions inappropriate to the dialogue e.g.: The naked man swinging a blood and gore encrusted broadsword jumped at me and screamed, "Where is your library card?" Possible, but not likely.

Characters can break in on one another. Especially if it's a mystery where emotions can run high.

A character might have a signature thing they say. People often do. Ever been in a classroom where the students mock the over-used phrases the teacher utters? Yup. Or watch a few sports interviews– "I'm just glad I could help the team" etc. etc. etc. etc. ad naseum.

Also be careful about questions and answers in a mystery. If you've got a sleuth who goes to each suspect and asks, where were you, I was home, from when to when, ten to twelve, did you call the dead person, etc. Nope. You need to vary this or summarize this or switch it around or give the character some actions and emotions.

Dialect – unless you're Mark Twain, I wouldn't. Certainly be careful with it. Many authors simply say something like, Mrs. Jones talked with a heavy Zardosian accent, but then report what she said in intelligible dialogue.

Diatribes – well, sure, but I wouldn't do a lot of these. Really, an angry boss doesn't go on and on. They just fire the person and get on with it. An angry parent needs to catch his or her breath. Although as usual, if you've got a well-placed diatribe, revealing character, realistically portrayed, sure.

Cops talk and make cute corpse comments – see Ed McBain's 87th precinct mysteries for the best examples of these. The whole dead-person lets-be-solemn stuff, well, of course, but professionals who work with corpses day after day? How would they really talk and react? Do your research and make sure you get this right. Any profession is likely to have verbal idiosyncrasies. Be sure to get them right. A snippet from *The Big Bad City* by Ed McBain:

> "What is she, eighteen?" he said.
> "Nineteen," Monoghan said.
> "Barbarian takeover," Monroe said, and glanced at the girl's face. "What do you think, Doc?"
> "My immediate guess is strangulation," the ME said.
> "Was she raped?" Monroe asked.
> "Can't tell you that till we get her downtown."
> "Guys who strangle teenagers usually rape them first," Monroe said. "Hello, Carella."
> "Hello," Carella said.
> Brown noticed that neither of the Homicide detectives ever said hello to him, but maybe he was being overly sensitive. "Has that been your experience?" he asked. "That strangled teenagers are usually rape victims as well?"
> "That has been my experience, yes," Monroe said. "Most strangled teenagers have been violated first."

Yes, real cops would likely talk this way. Plus, we get thrown in the extra snippet that two of the detectives never say hello to Brown. An absence of greeting that gives us a hint about the relationship among these people.

Use *he said, she said*. Period and be done with it. Don't try to snazz it up. In fact, if the reader can tell who's talking without even that much, do leave it out. Although always, always, always be sure your reader knows who is talking.

**Things That Should Be Obvious**

Characters need to speak appropriately to who and what they are. You can, and should, reveal the character by how they speak. From 'ain't' to verbose elocution and the million places in between, we need to know who they are from how they talk. A writer can give us detailed description, but a smattering of precise dialogue is a joy to behold. One side note: if you have a bigoted moron and you want to reveal his character by having the bigoted moron say the 'n' word: you certainly have the right to use the word, it is certainly revealing, but please note I will not buy your book and/or I will stop reading your book and buy no more of them. I assume you want to sell books, right?

Characters should react to what other people say. Far too often (once is too many) I've read books where I say to myself, that's not how someone would react to that news or that bit of information. Now, lack of reaction could be a clue for your sleuth, but as always use this judiciously. And people often have different reactions to the same news. For the most brilliant example of that I've seen, read *A Murder is Announced* by Agatha Christie – especially the opening pages where characters are responding to the same snippet of information in the newspaper. Dear Agatha got this very, very right. From the opening:

"Archie," said Mrs. Easterbrook to her husband, "listen to this."

> Colonel Easterbrook paid no attention because he was already snorting with impatience over an article in *The Times*.
>
> "Trouble with these fellows is," he said, "that none of them knows the first thing about India! Not the first thing!"
>
> "I know, dear, I know."
>
> "If they did, they wouldn't write such piffle."
>
> "Yes, I know. Archie, do listen. A murder is announced and will take place...."

We know or suspect that Colonel Easterbrook has been snorting and ignoring his wife for the past umpteen years. And I would be loath to try to count the number of times Mrs. Easterbrook has said, "I know, dear, I know." But we know people like that, and they really do talk like that. And if we don't know them, they sound like plausible people, which is half the battle. The rest of the opening is just as deliciously brilliant. And isn't that what we want as writers?

# The Killer Instinct

# The Bloody Ends: Killer Openings, Killer Endings
## by Michael Allen Dymmoch

Have you ever considered writing to be magic? It is. Good writers create the illusion of entire worlds with characters living and breathing – or dying – in a specific time and place. If the illusion is complete and compelling, we as readers live there too, at least for a while.

Is writing sleight-of-hand or true magic? Perhaps it's a bit of both: craft and an inspired act of the imagination. Imagination is up to you, but you can learn the craft. In the discussion that follows, we'll examine the craft of hooking the reader from the beginning.

Magic. Every magic trick consists of three acts: "The Pledge," in which a seemingly real situation is set up; "The Turn," in which the initial reality is challenged; and "The Prestige," where all is set right again. A successful novel, play, or movie is a kind of magic trick with a similar structure, usually simplified as beginning, middle, and end. This three-act structure, which has been around since Aristotle defined it, persists because it works.

## The Pledge

Where do you start? At the beginning is the obvious answer, but is it necessary to *start* telling the story at the beginning? What about *Pulp Fiction*? Once you have an idea of beginning, middle and end, sometimes starting in the middle (*The Constant Gardener* by John Le Carre) or at the end (*In the Company of Liars* by David Ellis) can be even more effective. But wherever you begin the telling, the opening must "grab" the reader.

What *must* the beginning of a great story do? First, capture the reader's interest. Second, set up the situation, crime, or puzzle. Third, introduce characters. Fourth, give an indication of what sort of story it will be, i.e., cozy, humorous, literary, or noir. What a great opening *should also do* is present an opening image or theme and prefigure what's to come.

Several examples of openings that accomplish these objectives:

> I didn't reckon on no killing.
> *Contrary Blues*, John Billheimer

> *Florida Panhandle.*
> At the age of nine, Tara Evans was one of the youngest bank robbers in history.
> *47 Rules of Highly Effective Bank Robbers*, Troy Cook

> "I swear to tell the truth, the whole truth an' nothin' but the truth, so help me God. For the record my name is Ajax Deters – though I mostly go by Homer – an' I'm sheriff of Boone County."
> *Death in West Wheeling*, Michael Dymmoch

> When a high-powered rifle bullet hits living flesh it makes a distinctive- pow-WHOP-sound that is unmistakable even at tremendous distance.
> *Open Season*, C.J. Box

> I was struggling against more than wind and rain that night as I battled through the Cathedral Close, but I blamed my mood on the weather. This was not my idea of a proper English Christmas.
> *The Body in the Transept*, Jeanne Dams

> "It's gonna rain all over our dead guy," said Olson.
> *Homicide 69*, Sam Reaves

Reread these examples. This time, note how much information they contain in a few words. See how they set the tone for what's to come, and how they create the need to keep reading. Like "The Pledge" in a magic trick, the beginning of a mystery must catch or hook the reader. The hook, however baited, is an event or statement that arouses a curiosity sufficient to keep the reader turning pages.

Keep it brief. This means there are a number of things that shouldn't be included in the beginning. While you need to keep the narrative comprehensible, drop anything that isn't absolutely necessary.

The strongest urge for most beginning writers is to put the protagonist's entire history – the back story – and the protagonist's family and friends in the first chapter of a novel or the opening paragraphs of a short story. Fight the impulse. Until you've hooked your reader with an interesting character – in action – the reader *doesn't care* about your character's history, relationships, pets, or sleeping arrangements. Besides, unless it's shown in flashback, back story is narrative – telling, not showing. And the back story is usually another whole story. If it's worth going into great detail, it deserves its own book.

So how do you handle back story? Like salt in a recipe. Too much makes the dish inedible. Only the aspects of a character's past that explain the actions of the character in *this* story are relevant. And these should be sprinkled in *when* the revelation is something the reader needs to know. Withholding details of your character's history keeps your reader curious and leaves information to introduce in future books.

Something you may also leave out of the opening of your story – if you have the nerve and skill – is narrative. For example, *The Postman Always Rings Twice* reads like a screenplay in novel format.

Really great writers have even managed to dispense with the usual rules of punctuation, as in the following opening from Bret Easton Ellis's *American Psycho*:

"Abandon hope all ye who enter here" is scrawled in blood red lettering on the side of the Chemical Bank near the corner of Eleventh and First and is in print large enough to be seen from the back seat of the cab as it lurches forward in the traffic leaving Wall Street and just as Timothy Price notices the words a bus pulls up, the advertisement for Les Misérables on its side blocking his view, but Price who is with Pierce & Pierce and twenty-six doesn't seem to care because he tells the driver he will give him five dollars to turn up the radio, "Be My Baby" on WYNN, and the driver, black, not American, does so.

Don't complicate your task by using a voice alien to you. It'll come across as gimmicky.

Here are a few more examples of terrific beginnings. Analyze what makes them good hooks.

They threw me off the hay truck about noon.
*The Postman Always Rings Twice*, James M. Cain

The first small body was found by Tommy Chester one cold and drizzling afternoon two weeks before Christmas.
*A Grave Talent*, Laurie King

January, as usual, was meat locker cold, and the girl had already been missing for two days.
*Blood Hollow*, William Kent Krueger

The body floated eight feet above the sandy bottom, suspended in gelatinous green light, face down, as if studying the bottom.
*killer.app*, Barbara D'Amato

Maybe it was the goddamned suit. Tailor-made Italian silk, light and flimsy as shed snakeskin.
*Bordersnakes*, James Crumley

They were in one of the "I" states when Zeke told Isaac he had to ride in the trunk for a little while.

*By a Spider's Thread,* Laura Lippman

Lambert Fleming was barely fifteen years old – and trying very hard to fit in – on that bright, sad afternoon in October when he suddenly became invisible.

*Applaud the Hollow Ghost,* David J. Walker

The Flute Clan boy was the first to see it. He stopped and stared. "Somebody lost a boot," he said.

*The Dark Wind,* Tony Hillerman

I was in a deep sleep, alone aboard my houseboat, alone in the half acre of bed, alone in a sweaty dream of chase, fear and monstrous predators.

*The Dreadful Lemon Sky,* John D. MacDonald

The body lay face down, off the center of the clearing in a pool of bright early-afternoon sunlight. The usual jungle sounds were absent – pigs and monkeys, nameless birds.

*White Tiger,* Michael Allen Dymmoch

## The Turn

The Turn, or middle, or second act, I leave to others, since this chapter is about Killer Openings and Killer Endings. Suffice it to say that the middle must heighten tension as it advances the plot, and must lead toward an exciting climax and a satisfying conclusion.

## The Prestige

So where do you end your mystery? At the point at which the story is complete. Or, to continue the magic metaphor, when all has been set right again. What the ending *must* do is solve the mystery; resolve the conflict; wrap up all the loose ends – or most of them; restore balance, order, or justice, or at least, provide closure; and satisfy your reader. What a great ending *should also do* is bring the story full circle in some way, even if only with an oblique reference; comment on the theme; and sometimes something more. Let's look at a few examples:

> After his release from prison, he published a book under the title: A Dumb-ass's Guide to Bank Robbery. It was an international best seller.
> *47 Rules of Highly Effective Bank Robbers*, Troy Cook

> Sometimes it is a relief not to have a choice. I will have to get Meyer to explain this concept to me.
> *The Dreadful Lemon Sky*, John D. MacDonald

> In the end it was pretty much like that scene from *Raiders*. Only *I* didn't fall asleep.
> *Death in West Wheeling*, Michael Dymmoch

> Around the square, the remaining shops were closing, employees chattering down the sidewalks, last-minute shoppers slipping and sliding under the weight of bags and boxes. The fuzzy candy canes and reindeer, the fat light-bulbs, everything the same as it always was, as it always had been. Everything the same. Everything different. Everything.
> He climbed into his truck and headed home.
> *In the Bleak Midwinter*, Julia Spencer-Fleming

> He grinned down at her gravestone. "God knows you must be sick of me still hanging around you after all these years."
> Out of a still, clear day, the wind suddenly picked up.
> It bowed the grass in his direction, unaccountably lifting his spirits and making him think that maybe she hadn't minded his devotion, after all.
> *The Virgin of the Small Plains*, Nancy Pickard

To close the circle, to create that "something more," is difficult. The feeling the reader carries away depends to a great extent on how well the circle was drawn from the beginning. It is something well described by T. S Eliot in *Four Quartets*:

> We shall not cease from exploration
> And the end of all our exploring
> Will be to arrive where we started
> And know the place for the first time.

*The Shape of Snakes*, by Minette Walters, begins with Mad Annie: "I could never decide whether 'Mad Annie' was murdered because she was mad or because she was black." And the book comes around to Annie in the end: "But Sam just reached for my hand under the table and held it companionably while I pictured myself beside a river, watching the bodies of Annie's enemies float by . . ." Walters begins her story with Annie and ends it with an image of justice for her killers.

The last three lines of the nineteen-line sentence that closes *American Psycho*: ". . . and above one of the doors covered by red velvet drapes in Harry's is a sign and on the sign in letters that match the drapes' color are the words: THIS IS NOT AN EXIT" obliquely repeat the image mentioned in the first sentence: "Abandon hope all ye who enter here . . . scrawled in blood red lettering . . ." and alludes to the theme of hell. The graffiti quotes the sign above the gate of hell in Dante's *Inferno*. And the final words of the novel, "THIS IS NOT AN EXIT," allude to Jean-Paul Sartre's play, *No Exit*, famous for the line, "Hell is other people." The novel's protagonist is an anti-hero who is either a serial killer or a madman.

The final line of Tony Hillerman's *The Dark Wind*: "When he turned to look, it had already been lost in the darkness . . ." repeats the theme suggested by the title and expanded upon in the book – that antisocial behavior is a form of illness.

A simple but powerful example of the echoing of theme is Raymond Chandler's *The Long Goodbye*: "I never saw any of them again – except the cops. No way has yet been invented to say goodbye to them." Again, the title theme is repeated.

The opening paragraph of *The Fall*, by Michael Allen Dymmoch, suggests the sailor's old dictum, "Red sky in the morning, sailor's warning; red sky at night, sailor's delight," and foreshadows the conflict to come. "Bloodied by a crimson wash of sunrise, a peaceful army of occupation foraged beneath the naked oaks in Crestwood Park, skirting the abandoned tennis courts and playground." The final lines follow through on the theme of the sailor's ditty: "At sunset, they all watched the red disk slip from a lemon-ice sky, below an icy gold horizon. . . . In the red glow of the firelight, she could no longer see the blood on their hands."

The first line of William Landay's *Mission Flats*, presents a peaceful image of water: "On screen, a woman lounges on a rubber float, fingertips trailing in the water." The final line repeats the water image and conjures up a different idea of peace: "I will leave my clothes in the Bronco and walk right into that water, let it take me in and envelope me, and swim out to the center, stroke by stroke by stroke, to the deepest part."

Jay McInerney's novel isn't a crime novel, but it does contain a mystery and it brilliantly illustrates T. S. Eliot's observation about coming full circle. *Bright Lights, Big City* begins:

IT'S SIX A.M. DO YOU KNOW WHERE YOU ARE? You are not the kind of guy who would be at a place like this at this time of the morning. But here you are, and you cannot say that the terrain is entirely unfamiliar, although the details are fuzzy. You are at a nightclub talking to a girl with a shaved head. The club is either Heartbreak or the Lizard Lounge. All might come clear if you could just slip into the bathroom and do a little more Bolivian Marching Powder. Then again, it might not. A small voice inside you insists that this epidemic lack of clarity is a result of too much of that already.

The story concludes about the same time of day, having explored the previous year of the protagonist's life. "You get down on your knees and tear open the bag. The smell of warm dough envelopes you. The first bite sticks in your throat and you almost gag. You will have to go slowly. You will have to learn everything all over again."

The climax of a novel must be satisfying and consistent with what has gone before, but the final paragraphs or lines of the book are what the reader will take with him. If the end reiterates the theme and presents a final image that makes an impact, it will stay with the reader. And the story will resonate long after he has closed the book.

"Fuckin' endings, man, they weren't as easy as they looked."

*Get Shorty*, Elmore Leonard

## Intrigue, Machinations, and Mayhem

# Notes on Plot
by Terence Faherty

## Introduction

These thoughts about constructing plots and subplots are the product of my nearly twenty-year career as a mystery writer and of a lifetime of reading. I've always enjoyed reading other writers on writing and hearing them talk about it in person. This is especially true of the "craft" aspects of writing, of which plotting is one. That brings me to my first aside.

## A Short Defense of Plotting

The ability to plot well was once considered as important to the serious writer as the ability to draw well was to the serious painter or a gift for melody was to the serious composer. Times change and draftsmanship, catchy tunes, and intricate plots went out of style in the last century, at least as far as highbrow art was concerned.

E.M. Forster, an English novelist of that period, called plot an "atavistic" feature of fiction, meaning a throwback to an earlier, more primitive form of storytelling, like the tales told around campfires by our ancestors thousands of years ago. To me, the atavistic charge is nothing to be ashamed of. Far from it. I like the idea that what I'm doing, trying to construct an entertaining story, is the same thing Homer's great great-grandfather was doing.

Well constructed plots have always been popular with readers and have made a comeback in serious fiction in recent years. The draw of a good plot is one of the reasons mysteries and thrillers are often found on the bestseller lists. Plotting is an important skill for any writer to master. When the trapdoor springs when the reader least expects it, that's good plotting. When the last piece of the puzzle falls into place, allowing the reader to suddenly understand everything that has gone before, that's good plotting, too.

## A Definition of Plotting

It might be a good idea to define plotting. Some people think of it as the process of coming up with a story from a basic idea, and that's true. When Alfred Hitchcock decided he wanted to make a film that ended with a chase across the monuments at Mount Rushmore, his screenwriter, Ernest Lehman, worked backward from that idea and produced the script for the classic film *North by Northwest*. In her book *Plotting and Writing Suspense Fiction*, Patricia Highsmith calls this process development.

But plotting is more than just inventing a story. It can and should also be thought of as a way of manipulating a story. In *The Longman Guide to Intermediate and Advanced Fiction Writing*, Sarah Stone makes this distinction between story and plot. A story is a series of events in simple chronological order. A plot is the meaningful arrangement of events intended to achieve the author's intent. For example, you might have a ready-made story to write about from your own experience. Say it is the year your college roommate contracted cancer and died. You could tell that story chronologically, but it probably wouldn't have the same impact if you picked out high points to dramatize, summarized others, and played with time, perhaps starting with your roommate seriously ill before flashing back to the first warning signs. Those decisions are examples of plotting.

I write whodunits, mysteries in which the reader is invited to solve the crime along with the detective, so one of my intents is to fool the reader if possible. My approach to plotting, as laid out below, reflects this.

## Developing a Plot

If life hasn't provided a ready-made story to serve as the basis of your plot, you'll have to create one, through the process I mentioned earlier, the one Highsmith calls development. Some writers start the process with a striking setting or character or an initial incident. Some even start with a final incident, the climactic scene toward which they'll build. I tend to start with what I call a hook idea, something that grabs my attention and may grab the reader's as well. Although I write murder mysteries, the hook doesn't always involve a murder.

Types of hooks I've used include unexplainable events I think I can explain (this could be something as famous as the *Marie Celeste* mystery or something very personal), odd bits of scientific knowledge, odd historical facts, what ifs (intriguing contradictions to known history), unusual or never before used murder techniques, and inside information on an industry or occupation.

I use a journal to keep track of and develop my hook ideas. Sue Grafton calls her journal a letter she writes to herself, which perfectly describes my own journal writing experience. It's strictly between myself and me. It's a place to save ideas. It's a place to "blue sky," to kick around an idea, asking over and over the question "what if?" It's also a place to pat myself on the back for keeping with a project and hitting my daily word count.

## Plotting Backward As Well As Forward

When you listen to mystery writers talking about their work, you sometimes hear the phrase "plot backward from the crime." All this means is it's usually helpful to start with the murder and why it happened.

My favorite insight about the mystery plot is Dennis Porter's theory that every whodunit contains two stories, the hidden story and the open story. The open story is the one presented to the reader. It is the story of the detective's investigation. The hidden story is the one known only to the murderer and the writer, at least at the start of the book. The hidden story is the long trail of events that led to the murder. The investigation begins at the beginning of the open story and at the end of the hidden story. As the reader and detective move forward in time through open story, they are also moving backward in time through the hidden story. The book ends at the end of the open story, but this is also the beginning of the hidden story. That is, when the reader and detective have solved the crime, they have arrived at its first cause.

## Three Steps of Plotting

What Porter's theory tells me is that it is a good idea to work out the hidden story first. So I start by identifying the crime and its causes. That's step one.

Step Two is figuring out how my detective will solve it. (If it seems like I've skipped an important step, namely coming up with a detective in the first place, that's because creating a protagonist is outside the scope of an essay on plotting. Check the table of contents to see what other contributor may have covered that base.) Because I know the hidden story, I know what information my detective will have to find in order to understand the crime. So I try to think of who he'll have to question and where he'll have to go to get that information. In other words, I'm thinking about the supporting characters and settings of the story.

After I have a rough idea of how my detective will solve the crime, it's time for Step Three: figuring out how to keep him from solving it too quickly. In other words, I think of obstacles to put in the detective's path. In a short story, no obstacles beyond the puzzle itself may be needed. In a novel-length story, you'll probably want several. Here are a few of my favorite ways to fool the detective (and the reader): present information in misleading context, present information through misleading witnesses (people who are confused themselves or who have their own agendas or theories), use red herrings (false theories too compelling to resist), jumble the hidden story (have the detective discovery pieces of the hidden story out of their proper sequence).

Highsmith calls this whole process (the winnowing away of illogical or impossible solutions and the piling on of complications) "thickening." Scott Meredith, a very successful and influential literary agent who wrote a handbook on commercial fiction, *Writing to Sell*, believes the best complications are those of the hero's own making, that the hero's initial attempts to solve the problem should only make things worse, an interesting idea.

## Plotting Through Character

Meredith's notion that characters should create their own complications reminds me that it's time for another aside. Thinking about the crime first and the hidden and open stories are useful ways to organize a mystery, but never lose sight of the fact that the key to any plot is character. After all, mysteries and thrillers really aren't books about crime. They're books about people in bad situations. When I work out a story, I'm always asking myself what my hero would do next and why. (Or, in the case of the hidden story, what the murderer would do next and why.) Great plots come from placing characters you know well under the gun (often literally) and getting them to show you what they'd do. Great plots never come from telling your characters what they have to do, regardless of how they feel about it.

## Plot Structure

One of the things I think about as I plot a book is structure. The basic structure of a story, decreed by Aristotle but obvious to storytellers from kindergarten up, is beginning followed by middle followed by end. I think of this three-part structure as I lay out a story and of the specific role each one plays in a mystery.

Part One sets out the challenge, sets up the situation, and introduces the world of the story and its major characters. There are two basic formulas for the beginnings of murder mysteries: body on first page of (or very early in) Part One, and body on last page of (or very late in) Part One. A police procedural might start with the police being called in to investigate a recent murder (body on the first page). Or a private eye might be hired to do an apparently simple job like ransoming a stolen necklace, only to have things escalate into a killing (body on the last page). Either way, Part One states the problem, but more than that, it captures the readers' interest. Part One contains an incident that upsets the settled world of the story. (A murder is an obvious example.) The remainder of the story is an attempt to reestablish the lost order and balance. By the end of Part One, the protagonist should be committed in some personal way to solving the mystery. James Scott Bell in his *Plot & Structure* calls the end of Part One the "doorway of no return." By going through it, the protagonist commits himself to seeing things through to the end.

Part Two contains the bulk of the investigation, including missteps, confrontations, and setbacks. In terms of length, it is the longest of the three parts and may be equal in length to the other two combined. It is the place where, according to Lawrence Block, "doubts creep in." The protagonist, who is in some sort of conflict in every scene, begins to be worn down and to second-guess himself. Though long, this part cannot be slow. It should be a roller coaster of plot twists (including, perhaps, additional murders), red herrings, non-mystery subplots, and false solutions. The stakes go up for the protagonist, and may include his life or freedom. This part ends with another of Bell's doorways of no return. This one sets up the book's final, unavoidable confrontation.

Part Three contains the solution to the mystery and the resolution of some (but not necessarily all) of the non-mystery subplots. The ending of the story must make good on the promise of the first chapter, which is why Tony Hillerman advised against polishing the first chapter until the last chapter is written. The relationship between the two should be that tight. Part Three is the shortest of the three parts and the most emotionally charged. It can end with the climax of the plot or the climax can be followed by a "resolution scene," an emotional release following the tension of the climax. I like this sort of ending myself. Arriving at the solution to the mystery may not resolve all of the protagonist's problems. The resolution scene is a place to resolve these or a place for the protagonist to come to grips with the idea that some issues will never be resolved.

### Subplots

One way to get a manuscript to book length is to include multiple plots, your main mystery plot and one or more subplot. I'm not talking about the filler material some cozy writers use, the little visits with or updates on all the members of the protagonist's extended family (and pets) that Nancy Pickard once likened to a Christmas letter. I'm talking about little stories woven though the main one. An example could be the protagonist's relationship with a significant other, which may be affected (usually adversely) by the investigation. Or it could be some other mystery the detective or an associate is investigating (or failing to investigate, due to an obsession with the main plot). Or it could be some problem in the protagonist's life, such as the need to care for an elderly parent that has nothing to do with the mystery, beyond dividing the protagonist's attention. The important thing to remember, as Donald Maass, a literary agent and the author of *Writing the Breakout Novel*, notes, is that subplots are still plots. All the basic elements (turning points, doorways of no return, climaxes, etc.) apply. Maass also maintains that each subplot should affect the outcome of the main plot or comment on main themes of the book either by reinforcing them or providing a counterpoint to them. Nevertheless, subplots and main plots needn't be tied together too tightly. As Sarah Stone puts it, they should be "linked, not chained at the ankles." Stone compares the relationship of subplots to the main plot with figures in a photo, one in the foreground and the others well back.

On rare and special occasions, a subplot may jump into the foreground. This happens when an ancillary investigation turns out to have a connection to the main one or a story thread involving the protagonist's private life becomes tangled in the main plot. You should be careful with this technique since its overuse will strain credibility and cause readers to be on the lookout for it.

## A Parting Aside

My final piece of advice and the most important one (hence the approaching exclamation point) is this: Remember to tell a good story! Analyzing plotting can make it seem as though storytelling is related to engineer-ing. It isn't, of course. What I've described are techniques I use to help me keep complex stories on track. But as I noted earlier, all good plotting comes from living, breathing characters reacting to life-or-death situations, not from formulas or recipes. Use any techniques that work for you to get the book laid out and written, but never forget that you're a storyteller, first and foremost!

# D. O. A.

# Avoiding D.O.A:
# How to Pace Your Mystery So the Reader Doesn't Check Out Early
### by Sharon Short

As readers, we've all faced this problem: we pick up a mystery novel, intrigued by the premise. We read for a page or two, maybe even a chapter or two, and then suddenly we come to a dead stop.

Or, rather, the story comes to a dead stop. Oh sure, it looks as though things are happening – suspects are being interviewed, bullets or machetes or poisoned pies may be flying, the detective is thinking and pontificating, characters are having tea or scotch or, perhaps, scotch in their tea – but somehow, we feel in our bones that the story has stalled out.

We've covered this ground already. Or we sense that these scenes just aren't going to lead us anywhere.

And we wish to throw the book across the room. Sometimes, we do.

It's easy to identify pacing problems, as readers, in completed works of fiction.

It's much harder, as writers, to recognize when we've gotten ourselves into a sticky pacing mess as we're creating the story. And once we suspect we have, how to get out of it?

As the saying goes in other areas of life, the first step to solving a problem is to admit you have it. So, first, you have to figure out if your project has a pacing problem.

Don't be disheartened if it does. There are some specific steps to making sure your manuscript doesn't qualify as DOA due to pacing problems.

## Clues to Diagnosing and Identifying Pacing Problems

Just as detectives ask questions to gather clues and solve cases, you can ask yourself several questions to figure out if your manuscript is suffering from a pacing problem.

### Do you have a premise... or a plot?

A premise is: Luann, unhappy with her current lot in life, decides to become a middle-aged runaway.

A plot is: Luann, unhappy with her current lot in life, decides to become a middle-aged runaway. But before she can act on her plan, she must find a home for Muffy, her beloved but geriatric Welsh terrier. Unfortunately, Staci, who usually dog sits, is out of town. That's too bad, because Luann knows when Staci figures out that Luann is gone for good, Staci will adopt Muffy. But George, Staci's hunky brother, is filling in for her, so Luann leaves Muffy with him. However, at her hotel later that night, Luann learns that George is himself a runaway... from a prison... claiming he was really innocent in that burglary spree last spring. And now he's holding hostage all the dogs at his sister's kennel. Obviously, this foils Luann's plan to run away. She returns to town, but while attempting to spring Muffy, she becomes George's next hostage, a situation further complicated when...

You get the idea.

If you have just a premise, you can perhaps do a few opening scenes that are intriguing. But after that, if you insist on writing without knowing what must happen next, you'll start to, frankly, blather, writing scenes that might be pretty but don't add up to a plot... or a can't-put-it-down story. For example, one scene of Luann discussing her discontent over tea with her friend, Staci, gives readers the information we need.

But if the next scene is a variation of Luann sharing that with Rayjean, and the scene after that shows Luann running into Ellen at the grocery, and Ellen comments on how Luann just doesn't seem her usual perky self lately...

then your story now is bogged down in pacing that is too slow.

Does this mean you have to have a firm outline before you write in order to avoid pacing problems? You can, but I don't think it's necessary. If you aren't by nature an outliner, you can approach writing as a loop-de-loop process – you write awhile, then you plot, you write some more, and then you plot some more.

### Do you have a prologue?

Sometimes prologues are good, but more often than not, they are misused and become an excuse for avoiding the real work. It's actually pretty easy to write what seems to be a great, compelling prologue. But too often, prologues can come off as trite to the reader, especially in mysteries.

What's worse, prologues, in effect, force you to start your story twice. You have to hook your reader once, at the beginning of the prologue, and then again, at the beginning of chapter one.

Often, getting started with the right momentum is where writers have pacing problems. Getting the opening right helps set the pace – because that's where you hook readers, and also that's where you set up a tacit promise with your reader: I'm telling this kind of story – a slower-paced, gentler mystery, or a fast-paced thriller.

### Have you done lots of research… or created lots of "pre-work" such as character biographies… that you're eager to share?

Research and pre-work are important, but avoid the temptation to dump too much of this information into your story. Use ONLY what you have to.

One clue that you are "dumping" too much of this material is "idiot dialogue." For example:

> "Please do take good care of Muffy," Luann said to Staci. "As you know, she's a Welsh terrier, and Welsh terriers are prone to..." (followed by a lecture on Welsh terrier diseases.)

This is "idiot dialogue" because the writer is using dialogue as an excuse to lecture readers who might not know about Welsh terrier ailments. If Staci already knows all this about Welsh terriers, she doesn't need a lecture from Luann – unless the writer is trying to portray Luann as an insufferable bore, in which case the writer can leave out the lecture, and show Staci fidgeting as she tries to politely get Luann to hush, and just leave poor Muffy at the kennel.

If it is really necessary to the plot to share a detail about Muffy's medical woes – perhaps this is part of what later causes Luann to return home – then by all means, share that one detail. But just that one.

**Is the back story holding back your story?**

Back story – for example, the circumstances that led your protagonist to investigate a murder – is important. But don't stop the story to share it. For example, don't get to the end of page two and then stop the action with a major flashback, such as: "Luann remembered when she first realized she was restless in her role as wife, mother, and PTA president. It was a crisp fall day, and Luann was walking up the steps to Greengrove Jr. High – where all the PTA meetings were held, because that's where Luann herself had gone to junior high, back in the day when toe socks were the must-have fashion item and..."

Start further in than you think you should, and weave, weave, weave in the back story! Perhaps as Luann is checking into her hotel on the first night of her doomed runaway attempt, she notices a young girl wearing toe socks. Then you might allow Luann a brief memory of her first pair of toe socks and how, when she was that age, she swore she'd get out of Greengrove as soon as she was out of high school... and so on.

**Fixing the Pacing Problem**

Pacing problem traps abound, as I've described above. But, fortunately, there are several relatively simple techniques to help writers avoid or fix them.

**Do the math! (Part I.)**

How many functions should each chapter have? At LEAST these two:

> Move plot forward.
> Reveal character.

What's more, if you can subtly add in one of these, all the better:

> Evoke setting.
> Show (don't tell!) theme (which actually shouldn't be readily apparent until the end of the novel.)

Stories slow down too much when a chapter has only one of the above functions. Also, re-read your manuscript to make sure you aren't repeating functions, for example, revealing character in the same way over and over.

# Do the math! (Part II.)

Writing a novel is a marathon, not a sprint, so it helps to get a handle on what you're dealing with for the long haul, and break the journey into manageable chunks.

For example, if your traditional mystery novel is 70,000 to 80,000 words long:

Opening chapter can be set-up. (Private eye hired; problem introduced; body stumbled on.)

Next few chapters, through about a quarter of the novel, can be more build up and gathering of more clues and information.

Then the detective needs to encounter a major crisis. (Another murder? A shocking revelation that turns the investigation on its head?)

The detective reacts to this crisis, and then pro-actively goes about using the revelations from the crisis to continue with his or her detecting work.

Another major crisis occurs.

The finale is last few chapters, in which the detective figures out the solution to the crime in the opening, confronts the culprit(s); and dispatches the culprit(s) in some way.

Knowing how much space you have to work within can help you mitigate pacing problems; for example, knowing that you need to get to the first major crisis after about 10,000 or so words means that you will keep yourself in check from letting the opening go on too long.

Another technique for managing pacing is to realize that pacing is not one-speed-fits-all; a suspense novel might call for shorter, faster scenes, whereas a traditional mystery novel might call for longer scenes or a mix of shorter and longer scenes. The pace must fit your voice and style, but in all cases, remember that padding is for the walls of your writing space – not for your novel.

And when unsure, consult the first pacing "math" solution!

## On the other hand... sometimes it's good to take a break.

So far, this chapter has assumed that most pacing problems are an issue of the writer moving the story along too slowly.

While that's usually the case (at least in my reading – and writing – experience), sometimes writers move the story along too quickly.

Be sure that you don't pile on plot points just to make the story seem fast and exciting: a car chase, a shootout, a street fight, followed by a car chase, a shootout, and so on.

Readers need a break not just to get a breather in-between all that excitement, but also to learn more about the characters and their motivations.

For example, after showing Luann hurrying back to town, breaking into the kennel to try to save Muffy, and then getting kidnapped by George, don't skip straight to her managing her escape. After all that action, it is fine to at last let Luann reflect on her situation – perhaps the irony of being more trapped than ever in a place she wanted to escape, perhaps realizing that running away from her problems isn't going to solve them. Maybe she even remembers the day she and her husband and kids adopted Muffy. That memory not only shows the reader something about Luann and her character, but could also serve to give Luann an idea about how to outwit George. And then it's back to the action!

## Micropacing

This is a lot like micro-management, except it's a good thing.

It requires editing and revising your manuscript, going through it line by line, paragraph by paragraph. This is where writing becomes like jazz music. Good jazz music has a rhythm that just feels intuitively right. There is no step-by-step "how to" for achieving that just-right rhythm, though. Musicians – and writers – must develop a feel for that just-right rhythm. And the only way to do that is through a lot of reading and writing.

## In Conclusion

You can find the right pace for your manuscript, but remember, doing so requires patience and, yes, pacing yourself as a writer. These tips are meant to get you started in thinking about how to manage the pace of your own work. Finding the right pace means knowing your story inside and out – not just the plot points but the characters and theme. In other words, why you wanted to tell this particular story in the first place. Stick to that, revise where needed, and soon enough you – and your story – will hit the right stride.

## I Haven't Got a Clue!

# Research and Credibility
## by Beverle Graves Myers

Like any great novel, a mystery needs to be anchored in time and space and peopled with compelling characters. Readers expect to be swept into a believable world, whether your setting is a thirteenth-century monastery, a state-of-the-art DNA lab, or a space port on the third moon of the planet Dalek. Much of your writing may spring from your own experience, but the further you stray from what you know, the more formal research you will need to do to. For writers with contemporary settings, your research may focus on an unfamiliar skill, occupation or locality. Those delving into history will take a broader approach. Ideally, your research should provide direction, confidence, and depth for your writing. You may even pick up some useful plot ideas.

Where to start? Your earliest research efforts are likely to be untidy and far-reaching, and this isn't a bad thing. At this point, you're following your interests and getting to know your subject – rather like a flirtation. Enjoy and allow yourself plenty of time. As I got up to speed on eighteenth-century Venice for my Baroque Mystery series, I began with history textbooks to develop a basic understanding of Venice's government organization, social structure, and economic basis. Whenever I came upon a personality or situation that seemed intriguing, I delved deeper.

I also had specific questions begging for answers. Were there any wars going on? I intended to center my plot on an opera singer with a talent for sleuthing. Tito Amato would never be a soldier, but his country's military victories or reversals would certainly affect him and his family. What about plagues? Revolutions? Famous natural disasters? I knew errors of omission would be just as troubling as getting major facts wrong.

Helpful non-fiction and textbooks on a multitude of subjects can be found at used book stores and in library collections. They don't have to be college-level texts. Sometimes a juvenile textbook has just the right amount of information to give you the basics. For my series, I combed the history shelves. Your needs will differ. I once bought a criminology textbook I ran across at a yard sale because it contained such great information that could be worked into a short story or novel. Aimed at students who would be doing correctional work, it contained detailed information about the typical scams prisoners pull and tricks they will use to get special treatment from guards. Characters and plot points practically flew off the page.

Cruising the Internet is a good place to find overviews on literally anything. Just be certain you understand the possible biases and limitations of the site you've clicked on. You're looking for information that is accurate, object-ive, and up-to-date. University web pages, government sites, and those accessed through a library's research portal are generally trustworthy. But remember that even a site that carries an authoritative title and appearance can be filled with unsubstantiated material if anyone is allowed to post articles without editing or moderation. Never rely on just one site; make it habit to double-check crucial facts.

Writers who are researching places rather than time periods could start developing their knowledge foundation with maps, atlases, geography texts or travel books. There are so many different types of maps, the subject could be a chapter on its own. I'll mention two examples to provide some ideas. The Sanborn maps document buildings found in older American cities. Originating in 1867, these highly detailed maps were developed for fire insurance purposes. Need to study a block or neighborhood in New York of that period? The Sanborn maps can tell you the number of floors in the buildings, the location of stairways and exits, and the composition of the structure. If your setting is more rural, check out maps provided by your state's Department of Natural Resources. They'll inform you about topography, geological formations, even archeological sites.

I've touched on libraries several times. I can't say enough about what a wonderful writers' resource they are. Make friends with the person manning the reference desk at your local library branch, find out how to request a book through interlibrary loan, and check out your library system's website. Mine offers free access to many other useful sites that charge a fee if you are signing up as an individual. Every writing day, I fire up the Oxford English Dictionary to check the dates that words came into use and what their definition was in Tito's time. Priceless information!

Sources for Your Foundation:

Textbooks
Biographies
Travel books
Maps
Internet

Once I had the landscape and historical framework of eighteenth-century Venice down, I delved into prevailing ideas. If you don't want your characters to present themselves like contemporary Americans in fancy costumes, you must understand the mindset of your chosen time and place. I'm talking about religion, philosophy, folklore, common fears and desires, moral values, and expectations for livelihood and marriage. Of course, these won't be the same for all your characters. Depending on educational background, social status, and other factors, people living in the same place may hold very different ideas. Just reflect on our own society: imagine a visitor from another planet trying to comprehend red states and blue states.

Here's where memoirs and diaries come in. These sources represent "people" history, real individuals expressing their concerns, hopes and fears. Novels of the period can also give you a good sense of what life was like. Think of how much an Agatha Christie mystery reveals about British society during the years between the world wars. And don't forget newspapers and magazines if they're available. Read these from front to back. Great information can be gleaned from society pages, agony columns and classified ads.

Sources for More Depth:

> Memoirs and diaries
> Newspapers and magazines
> Novels and/or films of the period
> Museums
> Historic homes and working sites
> Archaeological excavations
> Oral histories from living persons
> Re-enactment weekends or festivals

Before I go any farther, a few words about authenticity and credibility are in order. There seem to be two schools of thought which are embodied in the following, often-quoted rules:

> Never let the facts get in the way of a good story.
> Never distort the actual facts in pursuit of plot or character development.

As long as you tell a compelling story, some readers will blithely follow wherever you lead and never care that the details of flora and fauna or of dress and comportment are wrong. It's fiction, right? Not a textbook! Then there are the readers who are jarred out of the narrative flow by any perceived anachronism or inaccuracy. Instead of turning pages to see what happens to your scintillating characters, they're staring into space, wondering what else you've gotten wrong. Or worse yet, throwing your book across the room in disgust.

My philosophy concerning accuracy is to be as informed about my subject as time and energy will allow. I'm constantly aware that my Baroque Mysteries are often a reader's introduction to the history of Venice and early opera. Many of them believe that because the books have been edited and published they must contain the gospel truth, so I strive to get all aspects of the setting right, even though this level of research eats up a lot of my writing time. As long as something *could have* happened as I wrote it, as long as my story meshes with historical fact and the mindset of the era, then I feel at peace with my work. Doing it any other way just feels sloppy and dishonest to me. You decide how you want to play it.

A related issue concerns what readers think they know and what strikes them as incorrect even though you have good evidence to the contrary. One example: in a novel set in the 1740's, I once used "Frog" as an unflattering epithet for a Frenchman. Several readers wrote to assure me that the expression didn't come into use until World War II or World War I or some other time that they were absolutely sure of. My research indicated that when the British and French armies faced each other in the varied and complicated wars of the eighteenth century (anybody out there remember the War of Jenkins Ear?), the French saw the Brits eating tinned beef and dubbed them "Les Rosbifs." The French were eating frog legs, hence the nickname. There's no ironclad way to guard your work against this sort of thing, though having a few trusted first readers provide candid feedback on your manuscript can help.

Bottom line: do your homework and realize that you will always receive a certain amount of criticism.

Now on to the details. You've set your novel in contemporary India and your character wants to buy a snack from a street vendor. What's available for him to eat? How will he pay for it? Or my singer-sleuth Tito must take a journey from Venice to Rome in 1742. Does he go by carriage or coach? Perhaps he travels by water part of the way. How much does it cost? How long does it take? This level of detail is difficult to give advice on because the needs of your particular stories will be so varied, but several important points spring to mind.

The first is to never take any trivial item for granted. Everything came into use at a certain time, and you must discover that time. Remember the reader who threw the book across the room. If you have character light a fire with a sulfur match in 1731, you're asking for it. Ditto for moving an interstate highway bridge fifty miles one direction or the other. People who live in the areas you're writing about especially take offense when you make mistakes which could have been easily researched.

The Internet helps tremendously with these sorts of questions, but you have to know how to use Google and other search engines effectively. Hone down the number of hits by using the site's advanced features to combine terms or exclude non-pertinent items. You can also type quotation marks around words to search for them in that exact order. There is a certain zen to searching topics that don't lend themselves to simple key words. I've found success by jotting notes about the ideal article that would provide the information I need; then I search a few of the phrases I've come up with. It's a skill that improves with practice.

Also on the topic of small questions: don't discount the old-fashioned method of simply asking an expert. I've posed questions to university professors, clockmakers, carriage drivers, theater costumers, and many more.

Authors of contemporary mysteries often consult the resource officer at their local law enforcement district for details on firearms or police procedure. Most experts are quite willing to help if you identify yourself politely and respect their time. That means becoming familiar with the basics and making a list of exactly what you need to know before you make the call or send the email. Never expect someone else to do your research for you – unless you've hired them for that purpose, of course.

The third point is to make an on-site visit if possible. Reading about a place can't compare with personally experiencing the same sights, smells, and sounds as your characters. While in Venice, I picked up some little gems that I would never have imagined and had never heard anyone else mention. One was the way gondoliers propel their boats down the very narrow canals. If a boat is halted by oncoming traffic, the gondolier gets moving again by not only pushing on his oar, but also kicking out a foot and pushing off from the nearest building.

A few places to look for nitty-gritty details are listed below. The possibilities are nearly endless.

Sources for Further Detail:

Artwork of the period, especially the figures/activities in the background
Genealogical records
Vintage or local cookbooks
Old catalogues
Field guides to plants, birds, other animals
City directories and old telephone books
Collectors of coins, china, firearms, etc
Antique shops
Foreign language dictionaries
Specific texts, such as the history of transportation
Technical manuals

PhD dissertations (available at university libraries and online)

Now you're an expert. You may be having so much fun researching that you're loathe to face the keyboard, but when your plot begins to develop some structure and you're itching to tell the tale, it's time to write. I'll start with a caution about making your sleuth or another major character a real person. A few authors have used this device with some success; others have found they'd bitten off more than they wanted to chew. The more famous the character, the more completely his or her life has been documented and the less "free" time you have to work with. Readers may also feel that they "know" this character and are unwilling to give up their predetermined opinion.

If you've fallen in love with the idea of doing a mystery that involves Thomas Jefferson, for instance, consider using a little known or totally fictitious person as your point of view character. Perhaps Jefferson's secretary, plantation steward or heretofore unknown bastard son. The great man can do "walk-ons" in scenes that don't conflict with his documented activities. You can also create new characters based on historic figures by changing names and identifying characteristics or by melding several characters into one.

So, how do you use all the wonderful research you've done? The temptation is to communicate it all to the reader as fully and quickly as possible. This approach leads to wordy, awkward passages of exposition, sometimes called "info dumps." These are particularly tiresome when one character is explaining background information to another character who should already be aware of it. Remember, readers have opened the pages of your book for a story. Don't overwhelm them with detail. Include only those bits of information that are necessary for plot or characterization.

By working background into action or dialogue, you can force the fruits of your research to do double duty. On one level, a character's dress could be a simple recounting of clothing items, but dress can also convey so much more. Say you're writing a novel set in ancient Rome where men of substance wear togas. Your sleuth character meets someone whose finely woven toga is frayed at the bottom and sits on his shoulders a little too loosely. The sleuth might conclude he's meeting a slave who has inherited a cast-off toga from his master, a particularly cherished slave because the garment was once so costly. Author Steven Saylor opened one of his Gordianus the Finder mysteries in just such a manner. The scene stayed with me because it revealed so much about the characters and made them come alive.

When I'm describing a scene, picture it like a still shot from a film. What are the top two or three things that stand out for you? Those are what you use in description, not ignoring smells and sounds in addition to the visual. If you use this method and find yourself in doubt about including something, remember that every scene, paragraph, and sentence should have a purpose. If the only purpose you can come up with is, "But it's so interesting," then you need to hit the delete button.

A few other tidbits about research: Please keep a good record. All writers have their own organizational method, and none is inherently better than another. Whether you prefer digital files, a neatly indexed binder, or note cards taped to the wall, the trick is to keep your system up to date. When information is coming thick and fast, it's easy to forget where you found a certain phrase or fact. At a bare minimum, keep a list of all the books and websites you consult including the basic topic each one addresses. And believe me, page numbers for those crucial facts will come in handy later on. Also keep a list of people who've helped you. New questions almost always pop up as you write and, of course, you'll want to thank them in your acknowledgments. Another thing I wish I'd done from the beginning: as you work through your research material, make notes of possible character names, place names, etc. It saves a lot of time in the end.

An Author's Note can also be a valuable tool. If you've deviated from the historical record or taken liberties with a locale, here's a place to explain why and to set the record factually straight. All the interesting bits that didn't make it into the completed manuscript can find a home in the Author's Note, as well as a list of recommended books for readers interested in even more background information. Some authors recount stories of problems or colorful individuals they encountered in on-site research. Others explain what led them to be interested in a certain subject in the first place. An Author's Note is just that – anything you'd like to tell the reader is fair game.

In conclusion, I want to remind you that readers are on your side from the beginning. They want to be entertained, and if you deliver a good story that says something true about people and their relationships, they will loyally follow you through an entire mystery series. Don't shake your readers' trust and delight in your work by making mistakes that could have been headed off with some good, solid research.

# Breaking and Entering

# Marketing Your Manuscript
### by Kit Ehrman and Tony Perona

*Congratulations!* You've completed your manuscript and now you have only to get it into the hands of someone who can do something with it, and magically, it will become a bestseller. The hard part is over, right?

Published authors would love to be able to tell you that yes, the hard part is over. But you wouldn't want us to lie to you, and we would be wrong to mislead you. The truth is: the next part is every bit as much work as writing the manuscript. We can testify from experience that, for many, the hardest part of the journey from neophyte writer to published author is just beginning. Sometimes authors who write well have trouble marketing their manuscripts.

That's not meant to discourage you. If anything, we want to fortify you for the task ahead. And the good news is, we've been there, and we've done it. Maybe we're not bestsellers, but we have successfully been published by companies that paid us for our work, sent us royalty checks, and got our books to libraries and bookstores. There's no reason to think you can't do otherwise.

Before we start giving you the lowdown, let's take one more look at that manuscript you've completed. Here are a couple of key points to make sure you've addressed.

## A Last Look at the First Manuscript

First, did you write for yourself? Remember that the most convincing book you can write is the one you felt compelled to write. Don't write for trends.

Second, how's the grammar? I don't mean that editors will reject a manuscript on the basis of a few stray commas, a missing word here or there, or the occasional misuse of 'it's' versus 'its.' But here's the point – if your manuscript isn't fairly clean, editors or first readers will wonder about the author. If he/she can't construct proper sentences or doesn't know the difference between 'there' and 'their,' editors might wonder why they should read any further. So, be sure the manuscript makes the best first impression possible.

Third, as wonderful as the middle of the book and the last chapters may be, the most important chapters are, in order of importance: Chapter One, Chapter Two, and Chapter Three. That's because, in all likelihood, those are the ones editors will see. If they like Chapter One, they'll move on to Chapter Two. If they like that chapter, they'll move on to Chapter Three. If they like that one, they'll request the whole manuscript. Ask yourself: in these opening chapters, have I grabbed the reader, introduced them to the plot, and made a compelling reason for them to finish the book? If you haven't, then go back and work on that.

**The Hard Facts about Getting Through to Publishers**

A big publisher may have 20 to 22 readers who evaluate query letters and may look at manuscripts that come in. And when 1,000 submissions come in every week, not many are read. If you follow all the rules AND do everything right, they might open it, they might scan it.

Do you need an agent? Well, agents are as hard to get as editors, but once you have one, you have someone who can get your manuscript through the door and will probably get you a better deal in the long run.

No matter which way you decide to go, the sheer volume of queries crossing agent and editor desks is daunting. Years of experience allow these professionals to quickly spot convoluted plots, logic inconsistencies, insufficient character motivation, unpublishable lengths, and other reasons for instant rejection that occur when an author markets a manuscript before it's ready. Agents and editors are also experts at spotting compelling story ideas and skillful writing. You can't control rejections based on the agent or editor's personal taste, but you can learn to craft queries that are well written and will attract the interest of an agent or editor who does like your story idea.

The tools you'll need: the best query letter you can write, a damn fine one-page synopsis, and those first three chapters that you polished and polished.

## The Query Letter

Your marketing efforts will demand the best from your *nonfiction* writing. A query's sole purpose is to gain a request to see the manuscript. Even a query showcases the writer's style.

A query letter (a letter of inquiry) and a synopsis (a summary of the novel) demand that you think in terms of sales. This is what the editor/agent is looking for and contains the following:

1. the agent or editor's correct name, title, and address
2. a 'grabber' with an interesting first paragraph that briefly tells them what your book is about while at the same time showcasing your writing
3. a very brief synopsis in the body of the query letter
4. an explanation as to why you can write this particular book
5. explanation of the target audience
6. a brief indication of writing accomplishments (skip this if you don't have any)
7. a statement that the book is finished
8. a closing that thanks the editor or agent
9. a SASE (self-addressed, stamped envelope)

At this point DO NOT worry about simultaneous submissions. Keep your query letter to one page. Following are two examples:

*[Letterhead with all your contact information including e-mail address]*

April 11, 2001

Laura Blake Peters *[Address to individual, check spelling.]*
Curtis Brown, Ltd.
Ten Astor Place
New York, NY 10003

Dear Ms. Peters,

Visit a horse barn in the middle of the night enough times, and you're bound to run into something bad. A horse down in its stall, eyes clouded with the pain of colic, vapor curling in tendrils from its sweat-drenched coat. A cast horse, legs wedged against the wooden stall planks, withers cutting ruts in the sawdust with the effort to rise. A broken leg. Every horseman knows it. *[Catch their interest, show how you write and flavor of the book.]*

What you don't expect, what Steve Cline doesn't expect, is to find yourself in a fight for your life. But that's exactly what happens when Steve interrupts a horse theft and is caught up in a web of greed, lust, and jealousy. Insurance scams, forced buyouts, and murder simmer beneath the surface of an otherwise pastoral setting in my mystery/suspense novel AT RISK. *[Give them an IDEA of what the book's about.]*

After working on horse farms and racetracks for more years than I care to remember, this completed manuscript of approximately 95,000 words, and its sequel, are rich in the kind of detail and atmosphere that would appeal to many of Dick Francis's fans. *[Demonstrate why YOU can write this book, include word count and the fact that the ms is complete, describe target audience.]*

In 1999, I received a full scholarship to the Midwest Writers Workshop, and I've placed well in numerous writing contests, including the 1999 *Writer's Digest* Writing Competition which received over 14,000 entries. *[Writing accomplishments, if none, leave out.]*

Thank you for your consideration. I look forward to hearing from you. *[Always thank them and sound confident that you expect to hear back.]*

Sincerely,

Kit Ehrman

And:

Tony Perona
7892 Fake Address Drive
Plainfield, Indiana 46168
(317) 555-1212
aapperona@fakeyahooemail.com

December 4, 1998

Jane Chelius Literary Agency
548 Second Street
Brooklyn, NY 11215

Dear Ms. Chelius:

Last summer CNN, Tom Brokaw, Dan Rather and Peter Jennings all covered the reputed appearance of the Virgin Mary on the glass facade of a Florida office building. For months afterward its parking lot thronged with the curious and the believers. *[At the time, this would have been easily recalled by an agent. It was a big deal on television.]*

There are more than 50 such sites throughout the world, nearly half of them in small towns in the United States. While it seems cynical to think of the economic impact such appearances have on a community, the reality is – it's huge. Perhaps enough to kill for. *[Links current event to murder.]*

My mystery novel, *Second Advent*, deals with the fatal repercussions of just such an occurrence in the Italian-American community of Clinton, Indiana. Nick Bertetto, a former investigative reporter, is contacted by the parish priest to look into the puzzling death of the town's patriarch. Soon Nick finds the death is connected to the old man's involvement with a religious group spawned by reports of a divine apparition. Because Nick traded in his former job to do freelance writing and be a stay-at-home dad, no sooner do the murders begin to accumulate when Nick wishes he could stop sorting suspects and go back to sorting laundry. *[Gives them a sense of the book.]*

*Second Advent* is an 80,000 word 'cozy' mystery whose sleuth does his best to juggle potty-training, editorial deadlines and deadly secrets. Like Nick, I traded in my job (PR/ad exec with General Motors) and regular paycheck for regular hugs as a stay-at-home dad.

I am a published writer (former newspaper correspondent and columnist), and my work for General Motors included print, audio and video that was used worldwide. If this project interests you, I'd be happy to send you as much or as little of the manuscript as you'd like to see. I've enclosed an SASE for your convenience, and I look forward to hearing from you.

Sincerely,

Tony Perona

## Parts of a Query Letter

### Lead

A successful lead captures the reader's attention. You can open with a creative lead or a business lead. A creative opening showcases your writing style and skill while giving a feeling for what the book is about. Although creative openings involve greater risk, they may be the best approach for a writer who lacks publishing credits. Business leads are straightforward and inform the reader about a manuscript without any attempt to dazzle. Business leads may open with a referral, author credentials, or specifics about the book.

### Specifics about the Book

Agents appreciate knowing the details of the book (genre, sub-genre, setting and time period, central conflict) immediately. It saves them time and pre-qualifies you – or allows instant rejection – with agents who know right away whether they're interested in the kind of book you're pitching. If your book specifics meet their requirements, they will be more attentive as they read the rest of the query.

### Author Credentials

If you have impressive credentials or have won significant awards, open your business lead with that. Credentials indicate professionalism and hopefully guarantee quality writing. Grants, awards, and prior publications indicate that you are a professional. If you don't feel they're significant enough to open with, use them in the paragraph about the author; however, if an award relates directly to the manuscript you're submitting, this is too important *not* to feature in the opening line.

### Referrals

If you've had a previous discussion with the agent or editor about the manuscript, open with a reference to that discussion. Or, if you were referred to the agent by another professional in the industry, open with that.

### Comparisons with Other Books

Comparing yourself to other published writers is tricky but absolutely essential. A comparison will help the agent or editor immediately categorize your work, and this comparison can be used to pre-sell your manuscript to the publishing house. A comparison also sends a message that you know the industry.

Write several leads for your query and select the best. If you don't think you can pull off a creative lead, stick to the business lead. Follow with strong writing in the body and make every word count.

### Body

If your lead has done its job, you have secured reader attention. The primary element in the body is a very short (two or three sentence) synopsis of the story.

### Additional Query Body Information

The body should also include biographical information and any life experience that is relevant to your manuscript. Keep it short. Do *not* include testimonials from family or friends or critique partners.

### Closing

Every query should close with a handshake. "Thanks for your consideration. I look forward to hearing from you." shows that you're confident and expect a reply.

**Additional Thoughts on Sending the Query Letter**

While the standard query letter is a one to two-page document the query package is an expanded version and should only be sent to agents who require it for the initial exchange. It features a one-page standard query, a one or two-page synopsis, and the first chapter. *Be sure to read the agent or publisher's requirements before sending a package.* Some may specify three chapters. Some may not want a package at all but only the standard query letter.

A caution on using unconventional queries:

Don't use colored paper, perfume, etc. Don't send gifts. Keep it professional. That said, unconventional queries can work but can just as easily backfire. Read J.A. Konrath's tips article about how he secured an agent and a six-figure deal using an unconventional query:
http://www.jakonrath.com/tips8.html.
Also, check out his site for wonderful writing tips: http://www.jakonrath.com/index.html.

**E-mail Queries**

Don't use them unless invited to do so. Many editors and agents are moving into the electronic age, but it's an evolving process so check first.

**Oral Queries/Elevator Pitch**

Oral queries are used at conferences or during a telephone pitch. The foundation of every oral query is a synopsis, be that one line, one paragraph, or one page. The query – the most important piece of paper you'll ever write – can be challenging, but with practice and revision, you can make it look easy. See our separate section on 'elevator pitches.'

## An Agent's Perspective

Talent is everywhere.

In your query letter or verbal pitch at a conference or over the phone, you need to answer the question: *Why does the world need this book?*

You need to make your platform clear. Platform equals the quantity of books the publisher thinks she can sell. The agent and editor will look at your work ONLY in terms of how they think they can sell your book. You need to make your platform clear in your query letter *by stating who your readers are.* This may be as simple as stating "This book will appeal to fans of Dick Francis" or by explaining the professional organizations you belong to where the book will be popular.

Do not refer to your protagonist by the word protagonist in the query letter. Name him or her. Show, don't tell. You must get the agent to say, I want to know more. Don't refer to your manuscript (ms) as a book. It's not a book until it's a book. Make the agent believe you finished the ms yesterday. If it's been languishing for three years or going through the submission process for three years, the agent is not going to be interested.

Look at movie trailers for inspiration. Your query letter must include the following information in a compelling way: setting (year, geographical), protagonist, problem, voice. The agent wants to know right away, "Where are you taking me?" Agents are looking for INSIDERS. They want insider information. Either you've worked the job or you've researched it thoroughly. Start with, "Did you know?" and you're on your way to hooking them.

Put the big guns up front. If it's voice, showcase that first. If you have an incredibly strong platform where you expect to sell 40,000 books, put that first. When you indicate your platform through what's out there, include both author and book title, and don't forget movies.

They may want you to have the ms edited by a substantive editor. When the ms goes to the editor, the editor has to sell the ms to marketing, publicity, and editorial staff. Today's editors are product managers. They are evaluated on sales numbers alone and will be fired if their numbers are not good enough.

**Questions to Ask an Interested Agent:**

When an agent is interested in taking you on, you should ask questions:

> How have you done with works like mine?
> What's your prognosis for my career?
> What is your strategy for selling the ms?
> How do you like to work or be contacted?
> Are you the person to handle my submissions?

Publishers treat the mid-list book using the spaghetti method. Throw it against the wall and see what sticks.

**The Synopsis**

Some authors say writing the synopsis is more difficult than writing the book. The synopsis is basically a short plot summary, usually double-spaced and written in present tense. You must summarize the beginning, middle, and end, and you MUST tell how the story ends, even when you've written a mystery. The editor/agent needs to see that you were able to tie it all together. You need to illustrate the protagonist's efforts to reach the story goal (problem-conflict-resolution). It should be obvious that the story events happened because of who your characters are, especially your protagonist. A synopsis fails when it shows only a blow by blow account of what happened – the spy's cover is blown in the marketplace, he's chased through London's west end where he eludes his pursuers by ducking into a shop . . . This event-driven synopses is the type of story the editor/agent doesn't want. Plot that springs from the characters' wants and needs ensures that the story has a dramatic structure.

There are lots of good articles on the Internet about writing the synopsis. Keep your synopsis as short as possible. Make every word count. Use concrete nouns and interesting verbs. As much as humanly possible, eliminate to-be verbs.

Following are two examples:

FAT RISK: SYNOPSIS
by Kit Ehrman

Visit a horse barn in the middle of the night enough times, and you're bound to run into something bad. A horse down in its stall, eyes clouded with the pain of colic, vapor curling in tendrils from its sweat-drenched coat. A cast horse, legs wedged against the wooden stall planks, withers cutting ruts in the sawdust with the effort to rise. A broken leg. Every horseman knows it.

What you don't expect, what Stephen Cline doesn't expect, is to find yourself in a struggle for your life. But that's exactly what happens when Steve interrupts a horse theft and unwittingly crosses paths with a killer. After a harrowing ride in a horse trailer, accompanied by horses bound for slaughter, and a narrow escape, Steve returns to work and learns from the police that his case bears a remarkable resemblance to a horse theft that occurred six months earlier and resulted in murder.

*John Harrison's hay dealership is the only thing that's keeping his horse farm out of bankruptcy and Foxdale Farm's recent success is undermining everything he's worked so hard for. When Harrison's brother-in-law, Lawrence Timbrook, asks him to do what he can to destroy that success, because he wants to purchase the land for an upscale subdivision, Harrison doesn't need any prompting. He knows how to shake up a fancy show barn. Steal some of its horses, and the boarders will leave in droves.*

*He's done it before, to someone who's crossed him.*

An obnoxious horse trainer and difficult boarders, including a beautiful nymphomaniac, are easy enough to deal with, all part of the job. But when tack theft and vandalism plague the farm and the police investigation stalls, Steve starts an investigation of his own, utilizing his connections within the horse industry. As he moves closer to discovering the murderer's identity, the frequency of disturbing events escalates, and it becomes apparent that Steve is now the sole target as danger follows him home and heats up with attempted arson.

*Harrison finds this game of cat and mouse unexpectedly exhilarating. Exhilarating until he learns Steve is getting too close. He's not going to let a punk kid ruin everything.*

*It's time to put an end to the game.*

Steve's efforts pay off when he finds the trailer used in the horse theft. He connects it to Harrison and, through Harrison's sister, to Lawrence Timbrook's land development company, the same company that has been pressuring Foxdale's owner to sell. Before the police have a chance to act on the information, Steve walks into a cleverly-executed trap. He is able to get away, taking off through the woods on horseback, but Harrison anticipates his destination and tracks him down. In the end, Harrison's lust for violence and his overwhelming need to dominate are his undoing. Although Steve is shot, he gains control of the gun. Harrison doesn't think Steve has the guts to use it and makes his last, his final, mistake.

AT RISK is as much about dealing with physical danger as it is about coming to terms with one's vulnerability and strength of spirit.

SECOND ADVENT
By Tony Perona
~ 80,000 words

Synopsis

Former investigative reporter Nick Bertetto, now a stay-at-home dad, gets a strange call from the old hometown family priest. Believing the death of the town patriarch was not the suicide it appeared to be, Father 'Skip' Scipiannini and the patriarch's granddaughter, Martha Iavello, ask Bertetto to investigate. Nick is reluctant to take the case for personal reasons, but under pressure from Martha and with her offer of a large fee, Nick finally agrees to do so. However, no sooner is he on the job in the old Italian-American community of Clinton, Indiana, when he gets a warning to return home and stay away from Martha. As it becomes increasingly clear the patriarch's death was murder, Bertetto finds he must uncover the hidden secrets of the town's citizens.

There's no shortage of suspects for Nick to investigate. Martha Iavello, for one, has the most to gain from her grandfather's death. She is hooked up with Father Skip in a religious group called 'Children of the Second Advent,' to which half the patriarch's estate was bequeathed. The apparitions of 'Second Advent' are providing a mini-economic boom in Clinton, which could be expanded further with more money. Martha's brothers, Tom and Jimmy Iavello, are drawing battle lines over the will and had reasons to want the old man dead. Then there's Anna Veloche, Bertetto's former lover and now the local visionary, around whose message the 'Second Advent' organization revolves. Claiming the apparitions of a pregnant Virgin Mary signal the Second Coming of Christ, Veloche has a clear stake in the cash infusion the group gains from the patriarch's will.

And Pastor Carl Young, a smooth and smarmy faith healer, is also a suspect. He is at odds with 'Second Advent' and has a lot of influence in the area, most notably with the town's police force. Finally there are the area's angry and determined farmers, whose livelihoods may be threatened if the patriarch's family succeeds in completing the old man's scheme to sell off mineral rich land to a coal company.

Nick's investigation encounters increasingly disturbing events. The priest disappears. Tom Iavello dies. The pregnant Virgin Mary says she'll produce a miracle within three days. And Nick receives his own mysterious message from Mary. When Martha and Anna vanish amid the uncovering of evidence that they are responsible for two murders, Nick decides to head home. But the evidence appears to have been planted, and he is soon swept back into town rushing to his father's aid.

Nick views the projected miracle as his one chance to unravel the secrets of *Second Advent*. With all the players converging on the time and the place of the prophesied miracle, Nick finds hidden meanings in Mary's prophecy indicating the faith healer is behind the killings. Lacking evidence but determined to save Martha and Anna from being the next victims, he digs deep within himself and brings about the "miracle."

## Additional Tips for Writing a Synopsis

There is no single way to write a good synopsis. Here are some ideas that other writers have suggested about how to start, write, and conclude a synopsis, as well as what to include or exclude:

Does your book have a theme? Consider starting with it. (Or ending with it.)

What is your hook? (You do have one, don't you? Remember that first paragraph of your query letter… that's your hook). Consider starting with that.

Read your book and summarize each chapter in one or two lines.

Focus on your protagonist and describe what happens to him/her in the story.

Imagine your manuscript as a hardback novel. What would the dust jacket say to entice buyers to purchase the book? That's a synopsis of the book, written in an engaging manner, although dust jacket copy won't contain the ending.

You MUST tell the ending of your novel in your synopsis.

Mystery novels have suspects. Interest the editor with a paragraph or two explaining who they are and why they are suspects. (This works well with a puzzle-like mystery.) Or refer to clues that have been planted.

As far as formatting your synopsis is concerned:

Keep it to one page if you can, single-spaced. (Or two pages double-spaced.) Under no circumstances should the synopsis be more than 500 words. If the editor wants it longer than that, they'll let you know.

Keep the names you mention in the synopsis down to the smallest number you can. (If you reference them more than once, then it's probably best to name them.) Ditto with the names of places.

Write it in third person and use present tense. Use strong adjectives and verbs.

Your synopsis should reflect the book's narrative – if it's serious, so should be the synopsis, if it's 'chatty,' likewise. Use the same tone you use in the book.

Do NOT justify the synopsis so that the words are spread evenly across the page. Editors don't like to see that. Left justify your synopsis just as you would your manuscript and your query letter.

## Sample Chapters

If the publisher or agent accepts sample chapters along with the query and synopsis, they mean the FIRST chapters. Don't skip around. If you can't write a compelling beginning, no one will get as far as chapter four. Your opening should be worked over again and again until it's the best you can make it. Have other people read it and give you feedback. A good exercise is to read all the first chapters to your favorite books and see what works.

## Sending it Out

Use white, 20-pound paper. Make sure the type is clear and crisp. Courier New is the font most commonly used in manuscripts, but it prints light. If no font is specified, you may want to use Times New Roman, which prints out darker. But again, check your targeted agent or publisher's requirements. If a particular font is specified, use that. If not, use either Courier New or Times New Roman. They are the standards. Do NOT use a funky font, no matter how pretty or unusual you think it looks.

The standard manuscript word count average is 250 words per page. This is approximate and is easily achieved if you use Courier New or Times New Roman, double-spaced, with one-inch margins all around.

Single-space queries, cover letters, and short synopses. Double-space sample chapters and any synopsis over two pages long. Package the material so that it arrives neat and does not get bent. Include a SASE. Put clear tape over the packing labels so rain does not make the ink run. If the material has been requested by an editor or agent, print RE-QUESTED MATERIAL on the envelope. Sometimes they will give you a code word. If so, put that on the envelope.

## Who are You Going to Send it to, Anyway?

Find the right agent (or editor at a publishing house) by doing your research. The following books are excellent sources of information. Go through the current *Writer's Market* and select publishers who are looking for the type of book you've written. Check to make sure the name is spelled correctly. Check the title of the editor. Go to their website if they have one. Do NOT send a query to "Dear Editor."

Since you're going through books like the *Writer's Market*, make a thorough list of all the editors and agents who fit your qualifications and are looking for the kind of manuscript you're marketing. Will you need fifty or sixty names? Probably. In any event, it's best to have a good list. You don't want to have to go back and redo your research again and again if your top five agents or publishers reject you.

### Should I Send Out All My Query Letters at Once?

In a word: no. While you don't have to worry about simultaneous submissions right now, you also don't want to have a lot of agents or publishers requesting the manuscript at the same time, BECAUSE AGENTS AND PUBLISHERS WANT EXCLUSIVE RIGHTS TO CONSIDER THE MANUSCRIPT. Suppose, at their request, you mail off the manuscript to Harper Collins one day, and the next day get a request from Penguin Putnam to see the manuscript. Now you have to tell Penguin that Harper has it, and you'll be happy to send it to them if it gets rejected. Will Penguin want a rejected manuscript? Probably not, because they'll have less confidence, knowing it was rejected by another major house. Agents work the same way. Tony Perona lost a shot at Elmore Leonard's agent because he got trapped in such a quandary.

So here's a good rule of thumb: send out five queries at a time. When you receive three rejections back, send out another five. If you receive a request for a manuscript, hold up until you receive an answer back after sending out the manuscript.

### How Long Should I Wait for My Query or My Manuscript to Be Reviewed?

Query letters are usually handled fairly quickly, certainly within a month. If you haven't heard back within a month, the answer is probably 'no, thanks.'

A requested manuscript is different. A reputable agent or publisher should give you some kind of timeline. Three months or longer is typical. One way to handle this is to send a self-addressed stamped postcard with your manuscript. On the postcard, type a sentence that says something like,

> "We received your manuscript today and expect to have an answer to you no later than _____"
> Signed, _____.

The secretary to the agent or publisher will likely fill it out and drop it in the mail. You could always attach a sticky note to the postcard, saying, "Would  rest easier knowing you received this. Would you mind sending this back to me?" Then, when the time has passed, you can drop them a line and ask how things are coming. It helps to keep the dialog open between you and the person considering your work. Of course, if they keep missing deadlines they set for themselves, that should tell you something about how serious they are about your manuscript. Move it along to someone else.

### Other Ways to Get Your Foot in the Door

In today's market, getting published is extremely difficult. It takes perseverance, patience, and luck. There are other ways to break in.

Enter contests (many writers' conferences sponsor contests) try to find ones without entry fees
Search the Internet for contests
Work to get short stories published
Attend writers' conferences, especially where agents and/or editors will listen to pitches
Get to know some people: network

## The 'Elevator Pitch'

As mentioned above, one place to meet agents and editors is at writers' conferences, where they will sometimes allot special time slots for networking. But don't be afraid to approach them to make your pitch if the opportunity presents itself. My favorite elevator pitch story comes from writer Jeff Stone, who writes the Five Ancestor series aimed at middle grade readers. Jeff's pitch was extraordinarily successful. Here's a quick summary of how it came to be, and what his pitch was:

Jeff's idea for the Five Ancestor series included seven books, a large project he felt would be difficult to pitch to a publisher without an agent. After researching his options, he found a workshop sponsored by the Andrea Brown Agency. Andrea was a former editor and the first person to represent children's authors exclusively. She had a long-standing reputation, and the writers' workshop she was putting on was a great place to meet her.

At the conference he arrived early, determined who the players were, and approached Andrea Brown. His pitch went something like this: "My name is Jeff Stone, I've got an idea for an action/adventure martial arts series for middle grade readers. The premise is: it's set in China 350 years ago in a fictitious warrior monk temple, much like the Shoalin Temple. In the opening scene of the first book, the Temple is attacked and destroyed. The only survivors are five young warrior monks between the ages of eleven and thirteen. Each has already mastered a different style of animal kung fu that is consistent with both their personalities and their body types."

He only got through the first sentence of the pitch. Andrea called over her right hand woman, Laura Rennert, shouting across the room, "Hey, Laura, get over here and listen to this guy's pitch!" Out of that meeting came an auction with four publishing houses and a major contract for Jeff with Random House.

Keep in mind that Jeff also thoroughly researched the market. He was well prepared to further discuss his proposal with three sample chapters, five pages of marketing materials, a short synopsis of each book, and raw data about the number of kids in the U.S. (not to mention worldwide) who were taking martial arts.

But without that refined elevator pitch, the result of months of work, beating two paragraphs into one paragraph, and then into one sentence, he would never had gotten the agent's attention. Elevator pitches, done well, can be very effective.

(More information on Jeff and his series can be found at www.fiveancestors.com.)

# Patience, Persistence, and Practice
## by S. M. Harding

If I regret anything about my writing journey, it's sending out my first manuscript too early. During a long winter in northern New Mexico where the road over the mountains to the nearest bookstore was closed more often than not, I wrote to read a new book. I hadn't learned the craft, though I'd written non-fiction all my life. And I hadn't done my homework on the submission process.

It's amazing I ever got any agent responses, much less positive ones. But I did. I didn't get representation (no surprise in hindsight), but I got wonderful comment and advice from Jodie Rhodes, a west coast agent. Her advice? Find a good writing group or workshop and get feedback from other writers.

At the time, living twenty-five miles from the closest town, it was an impossibility. Online writing groups didn't exist yet, or at least I couldn't find them. But one of the first things I found on returning to Indianapolis was the Writers' Center of Indiana and a critique group that fit into my work schedule. I also took a series of workshops from Candace Denning through the Writers' Center. I still hear Candace's voice in my head when I write dialogue. I returned to the novel and rewrote it.

The advice I got from the writing group was helpful, except one piece: try reversing chapters one and two. In the intervening rewrites, I've realized that was the wrong advice. What they should have said was "Too much back story in the first chapter, take it out and dribble what's important into the rest of the novel." After several more rewrites, I came to that advice on my own, but only because I'd kept working at the craft and realized I needed the action in that old first chapter as an introduction to the story.

## Patience

Patience isn't passive. If you've finished that first novel, search your area for a writing group. If there aren't any, look online or ask an independent bookseller (particularly a mystery bookstore) and see if they might be interested in starting one. I gently pestered Jim Huang of The Mystery Company into forming one and advertising its genesis in the store's newsletter. Seven years later, we're still going. In the last four years or so, members of the group have had about sixty short stories published. Besides tangible success, the group is honest in critique and absolutely supportive of each writer.

You can also look for workshops, either through a local writers' center or through announcements in writers' magazines. From my own experience, Antioch Writers' Workshop in Yellow Springs, Ohio, is one of the best. They provide an intimate setting where writing is the focus for a week, authors "do" lunch and are generally accessible, and they welcome genre writers (which is not always true of other workshops).

And while you're searching for resources, see what kind of writing classes are available at local colleges and universities and their continuing education programs. Internet blogs like Murderati, Hey, There's a Dead Guy in the Living Room, Criminal Brief: The Short Story Project, and Backspace carry good conversations and tips about mystery writing.

Conferences can provide good instruction, too, if they're writer oriented as opposed to fan based. They offer panels of authors on writing and the business of writing, and speciality areas like forensics, police procedures, etc. Love Is Murder (on a Dark and Stormy Night) is an excellent one based in Chicago. Another mid-western site is Magna Cum Murder in Muncie, Indiana. But these kind of conferences flourish all over the country. And when you're ready, many offer pitch sessions with agents and editors. One note of caution: if you haven't finished at least a first draft, don't even think about pitching unless you just want the experience. Even then, you're risking an opportunity with an agent.

Organizations for writers can help enormously in gathering a network of contacts and finding good sources to learn the craft. Sisters in Crime is an international group with over forty local chapters in the United States. At local meetings, guest speakers can cover a variety of topics of interest to mystery writers. SinC also sponsors an online group for beginning writers called Guppies. Mystery Writers of America also provides a number of services for members. They are divided into eleven geographical area chapters. Both SinC and MWA publish newsletters.

Books and magazines on writing? There's a gaggle of them, many of them geared toward mystery writers. One book I always recommend is Ursula K. Le Guin's *Steering the Craft*. She not only examines slippery topics like voice and point of view (POV), but does so with concrete examples and exercises. Even for accomplished writers, she can get us out of the doldrums and help steer around the big rocks in the rapids. Magazines like *Writer's Digest* and *The Writer* provide craft tips in small doses, and *Poets and Writers* gives an extensive listing of workshops and writing programs in the last section. One of my favorite magazines is *Mystery Scene Magazine*. You won't learn craft, but you'll learn the business. When you've polished that manuscript to word-perfect precision and are ready to write a query letter, take a look at the reviews to see how to condense a novel into a hundred word description that's accurate yet intrigues.

## Persistence

Another part of the equation is persistence. There's the old saw "It takes ten years and writing four novels to get published." Says Brett Battles on the Murderati blog,

"Ultimately, it doesn't matter what the total is for the years and novels...The point isn't the numbers themselves, it's what they represent. And what they represent is the desire and the dedication to the craft of writing. What it means is that if you want it – want to be published – you can't give up. Persistence."

Persistence in continued improvement as well as in the face of rejection. Barbara D'Amato notes in the blog The Outfit: "English author John Creasey is said to have received 743 rejection slips before he got an acceptance and a publisher. . . How do you take 743 rejections? It is often said that being told your novel is no good is like being told your baby is ugly. Well, maybe. But usually when that happens you keep the baby. A writer may just give up."

**Practice**

How do you get to Carnegie Hall? Or in this case, to a published novel? Practice, practice, practice. Author Marcia Muller gives this advice: "Plant seat of pants on seat of chair in front of the computer or typewriter or stone tablet. Write something every day, even if it's only a one-sentence paragraph."

Life intervenes. Family or job emergencies, illness, disaster. Those should be the exceptions to establishing a regular writing habit. Find – no, *make* – some time each day to spend alone in your fictional world. Even if you end up polishing what you wrote yesterday, you're forming a thread of continuity. And before you close the file or legal pad, take notes on what you've written that includes plot points, character traits, or generally, who did or said what with whom and where. I promise, it will come in handy later – not only when you begin to write your synopsis, but when you need to find a certain scene to check details when you're writing two hundred pages away from that scene. You might want to do a spreadsheet with characters, locations, and main plot points for each chapter.

A wonderful way to practice is to attempt a short story and there are a number of reasons why. First, two to five thousand words is a very different investment in time and energy than sixty to one-hundred thousand. It's not instant gratification, though, except in relation to a novel. Second, the best way to improve writing skills is to try a form where every word counts. Anything extraneous to the story has to go. Third, short stories are a great way to learn how to plot. In a limited number of words, a crime must occur and its solution happen. Fourth, characterization and setting must be done in a few well-chosen strokes. While you may have to figure out the back story of your protagonist, you won't have the time to explore it in the short story. As with setting, pick out defining characteristics. Another benefit is to take your protagonist from a novel and throw her into a completely different world; you learn unexpected character traits that you never knew were there. Ditto with secondary characters from the novel.

The fifth is a practical one: if your story gets published, you've begun to establish your credentials for an agent or editor. Ten years ago, the mystery short story market was very limited. That's no longer true with a slew of magazines online or in print, as well as the growth of anthologies. Sixth is to pattern behavior when you write the novel. Let the story "rest" for a month (to gain some distance from the first flush of excitement), go back and edit or rewrite, share it with a writers' group or workshop, incorporate good suggestions for improvement, let it rest again, give it a final polish, send it out. Which happens to be the same routine to follow for a novel-length manuscript. Good practice all around.

Recently, I received a query from an agent – yes, you read that right. A well-known, solid New York agent. He'd read a short story that was published in *Spinetingler* and asked if I had a novel. We're still in correspondence, so I don't have an ending yet, but the point is, a short story did it.

So, the words I have taped to my computer screen are patience, persistence, practice. Right next to that is a quote from Denise Dietz: "If you drop a dream, it breaks."

# Writing Murder:
## A Matter of Fits and Starts
### by Phil Dunlap

Every writer's dream is to complete a fantastic novel, send it to the first agent in the *Writer's Market*, get it accepted with unfettered raves, see it sell after an auction to the second biggest publisher in the world for a $1 million advance and a 15-book contract. Hey, what's that noise? Oh, it's my alarm clock. Must have dozed off. Great dream, though, huh? But that's all it was: a dream.

Dreams are wonderful things to have. We must never stop dreaming. But a large dose of realism to temper our runaway egos will go a long way toward ultimately selling that book you've just finished, or at least have a healthy start on. If it isn't finished, or if you're still in the idea stage, where do you start? That's the real question, isn't it? And believe me when I say there are many starts ahead of you. You *start* with an idea; *start* writing; *start* revising; *start* editing; *start* looking for an agent or a publisher; *start* promoting/marketing. *Starts* are what it's all about.

Do I come up with an idea first, or do I just start writing and expect it will come spilling out of my subconscious, a wellspring of genius? Do I outline, or not? Is it going to be a mystery, romance, western, sci-fi, or…how about a romantic western mystery set on the planet Mars? Don't laugh; there are some of those out there. Of course *all* those decisions must be considered before anything can happen, but knowing *where* to start is the most important initial hurdle.

In my case, I started with a dare to myself. I'd just finished a paperback Western purchased in an airport bookstore. I read it in its entirety on the flight home. By the time I stormed in my front door, I was so certain I could write rings around that author that I started immediately plotting a story, with every intention of developing it into a full-blown novel. The plot concept came first, then I started writing from the beginning: Chapter One. Now, I couldn't imagine sitting down and writing a ninety-thousand-word novel without a hiccup, but I knew I had to start somewhere. Some authors start with an outline, I didn't; and after five published novels, and three more finished awaiting publication, I still don't. There's nothing wrong with outlining, it just doesn't fit with the way my mind works. In fact, over half of all published authors agree with me (Stephen King, for instance). So I just start and keep on writing until it's finished. Of course that's when the hard work begins: heavy-duty editing, revising, rewriting, and re-evaluating every scene, every chapter, every nuance to make it the best it can be. Add to that, the advisability of having another pair of eyes peruse your golden nugget.

The very first book I wrote failed to sell. That was years before the 'dare' novel. It made it into the hands of a well-known agent, but he said the time wasn't right. He gave up after four publishers. I put it in a drawer and pondered my next book. I wrote another and another and another. I didn't send any of them out, except that first one. Still haven't. As it turns out, they were great tools for learning the art of writing a novel. With each one, I learned a little more. When I wrote the book, *The Death of Desert Belle*, the 'dare' book, it sold to the second publisher I sent it to. That was the one I'd written with a twinge of anger at the writer of the book I'd read on the airplane, the one I thought was pure trash, and sent to the publisher who'd published it. They said no. So, I sent it out to another publisher who loved it, and bought it. Strangely, the very first book I'd written, the one rejected by an agent, and sitting at home in a drawer, turned into my second sale, *fourteen years* after I'd written it. That's *my* overnight success story.

Strangely, the publisher I sent *Desert Belle* to, the one that first turned it down, was the same publisher that bought the paperback rights to my second book, *Call of the*

*Gun,* which has since gone to large print with yet another publisher. Libraries across the country have been eagerly snatching up the large print version for which they have a large demand.

Making that first sale can be a huge hurdle that, once overcome, changes your life and your writing forever. Publishers almost never take a book they've received, and approved for purchase, without giving the author a significant editorial 'mugging.' Editors are a breed apart, and they have insights that differ greatly from our understanding of how books actually get to the shelves of a bookstore. Editors are not only trained in the fine art of correct English, punctuation, phrasing and spelling, but they also have that innate feel for what makes a good story, one that people will actually buy. Maybe even like, if you're lucky. That always helps when you are seeking acceptance for a second book.

A good editor can make you a better author, if you listen and comply with suggested revisions. The editor is your link to success. I've heard writers say, "Well, my editor made some suggestions, but I'm not going to change anything because I think she's wrong." That's a big mistake. We writers get close, very close, to our stories and sometimes that can result in tunnel vision. My first book was bought on the basis that I would agree to cut a few words to bring the overall length in line with the limitations of that publisher. It wasn't a big deal, actually, a mere 10,000 words. *10,000 words!* Good grief, how could I be expected to cut that much out? But I wanted to sell my book, so I dug in and started cutting. Guess what? After I had every last one of the 10,000 words eliminated (one heck of a lot of adjectives), I found that my story was tighter, moved better, and kept the reader engaged. Shorter chapters, each with a cliffhanger or a grabber to make the reader look forward to the next chapter, were things I learned and still use today. An editor was responsible for that. And I thank her over and over with each successive novel I write. So, write tight!

Another thing I had to learn early on was that getting an agent isn't a make or break situation. Sure I suppose an agent might get you into the big five publishing houses easier than you can yourself, but don't let not having an agent keep you from sending your query, sample chapters, or even full manuscript out. There are plenty of small and medium-sized publishing houses that don't care whether you have an agent. So, don't let that become a stumbling block. And don't forget, agents take fifteen-percent right off the top. After you've made a few sales all on your own, an agent is going to be more approachable. Bide your time, don't get panicky, and get that manuscript out there.

Another thing that trips up newer writers is trying to write a book based on what is popular today. The latest trend isn't going to *be* the latest trend by the time your book is finished, considered by several editors or agents, bought by a publisher, edited, prepared for printing, printed, and distributed to book stores. By then, the bloom has likely worn off that trendy little niche you sought to jump on, and your book will sell poorly, if at all. Write the novel you want to write or that you like to read. When you're ready, send it out. If that's not what editors are looking for at that time, wait (putting it in a drawer really does work). Then you'll be ready when the time is better. If you have a good story that is well written, someone out there will give it a fair read and probably snatch it up. Editors see so much garbage that they get a little cranky when they see just another so-so script from someone trying to hit the current trend. That's why it's so important to make your story the best it can be, something that will rise to the top of the slush pile and get noticed.

Oh, and don't forget to read, read, read. If you can't identify a great story, you won't be able to write one. That's a guarantee. That doesn't mean go out and copy the style of a Hemmingway or King or Clancy, whatever genre you prefer, but reading extensively in that genre will help you find a fit for your particular style. If you want to write horror, but have never read horror, good luck. Those manuscripts are destined to gather dust in your basement forever. Thorough research is your writing partner. People want to read stories that put them in the scene, in a particular time and place, and they want to feel that they are there as eyewitnesses to the action. It's your job to let the reader feel the searing heat of the desert, smell the decaying fish on a Boston wharf, or recoil at the sight of a bloody body torn apart by a mad killer. If you don't invite the reader into your world, they won't be tempted to stick with it to the end. And we all know that spells "no next book."

You can't put people in the scene if you are tentative with your facts, either. If you are telling a story about a man with an AK-47, you better know what one looks like, feels like when it's fired, how it spits out the empty shells, and how hard it kicks. Does it shoot flame from the end of the barrel? Can you put a silencer on a revolver? Could you actually conceal a shotgun under a raincoat? Better know the answers to questions like these because the reader will and they won't put up with wimpy generalities like, "He pulled the gun from his pocket and fired. His target fell to the ground and died. He ran from the scene leaving footprints on the street." What kind of gun, semi-automatic pistol, revolver, small-bore or large? Where was the victim hit, in the shoulder, heart or head? How did the shooter manage to leave footprints on the street – was it newly paved with asphalt, was it muddy, or was there snow? Don't leave your reader confused about the facts. And, you can only write the facts if you've researched them.

How to start? Prepare your mind for the task at hand. Ignore the prattle from those who know nothing about becoming an author. Turn off the television. Shut out the whining of those who say you won't make it. If writing is your dream, do it. It is a wonderful, rewarding, confidence-boosting experience. Read, read, read, write, write, write. And never give up!

## Additional Sources:

**Writing Technique:**

Ephron, Hallie, *Writing and Selling Your Mystery Novel*, Writers Digest Books, 2005.

Grafton, Sue, ed. *Writing Mysteries: A Handbook by the Mystery Writers of America* (2nd ed), Writers Digest Books, 2002.

Goldberg, Natalie, *Writing Down the Bones*, Shambhala Press, 1986.

King, Stephen, *On Writing*, Scribner, 2000.

Lamott, Anne, *Bird by Bird*, Anchor Books, 1995.

Le Guin, Ursula K., *Steering the Craft*, The Eighth Mountain Press, 1998.

Lerner, Betsy, *The Forest for the Trees: An Editor's Advice to Writers*, Riverhead Books, 2000.

Lukeman, Noah, *The First Five Pages: A Writer's Guide to Staying Out of the Rejection File*, Fireside Books, 2000.

Lyon, Elizabeth, *The Sell Your Novel Tool Kit*, A Perigee Book, 2002.

Roerden, Chris, *Don't Murder Your Mystery*, BellaRosa Books, 2006.

Shoup, Barbara and Margaret-Love Denman, *Novel Ideas; Contemporary Authors Share the Creative Process*, University of Georgia Press, 2nd edition, 2009

Strunk, William, Jr. and E. B. White, *The Elements of Style*, Allyn and Baco, 4th edition, 2000.

Wheat, Carolyn, *How to Write Killer Fiction*, Perseverance Press, 2003.

**Some Specific Recommendations:**

There are a good many books that give excellent advice to writers. Two I have found particularly useful are out of print, but worth seeking: *The Fiction Writer's Silent Partner*, by Martin Roth, ISBN 0-89819-482-X, and *Fiction*, by Michael Seidman, ISBN 0-938817-46-9. And

Carolyn Wheat's *How to Write Killer Fiction*, ISBN 1-880284-62-6, is I believe still in print, and is wonderful.
*Jeanne M. Dams*

For more detailed information on point of view, I'd like to recommend two excellent books. Both give advice on all aspects of novel writing and make handy quick reference guides. *Steering the Craft* by Ursula K. Le Guin is a must for bare-bones technique and style. *Manuscript Makeover* by Elizabeth Lyon is designed to strengthen and transform your work in revision.
*Mary Saums*

Carolyn Wheat: *How to Write Killer Fiction*; Almost half the book is devoted to writing suspense. It's been extremely helpful to me, especially her discussion of "The Four Outcomes."

Stephen King: *On Writing*. A wonderful refresher / review of what we should be doing. I like to listen to it in the car.

Anne Lamott: *Bird by Bird*. I love her discussion of "Shitty First Drafts." It's helped me get "unstuck" many times.

Francine Prose, *Reading Like A Writer*. A worthy tome that cites classic examples of each element of craft she deems important. I also love her list of "Books to Be read Immediately."
*Libby Fischer Hellmann*

*"Shut up!" He Explained* by William Noble – try libraries or used books stores for this out of print but helpful book.
*Mark Richard Zubro*

*The Complete Guide to Editing Your Fiction* by Michael Seidman

*Revision A Creative Approach to Writing and Rewriting Fiction* by David Michael Kaplan

*The Writer's Handbook for Editing & Revision* by Rick Wilber

*Self-Editing for Fiction Writers* by Rennie Browne and Dave King

*Making the Perfect Pitch: How to Catch a Literary Agent's Eye* by Katharine Sands.

*Kit Ehrman* and *Tony Perona*

## Reference Guides:

Roth, Martin, *The Crime Writer's Reference Guide*, Michael Wiese Productions, 2003.

Snow, Robert L., *Murder 101: Homicide and Its Investigation*, Praeger Publishers, 2005.

## Websites:

Sisters in Crime: www.sistersincrime.org

www.sistersincrimeindiana.org (local chapter)

Mystery Writers of America: www.mysterywriters.org

www.mwamidwest.org (Midwest chapter)

Mystery Scene Magazine:   www.mysteryscenemag.com

Crimespree Magazine:   www.crimespreemag.com

Agent Query:   www.agentquery.com

## Blogs:

Hey, There's a Dead Guy in the Living Room:

www.heydeadguy.typepad.com

Jungle Red Writers:   www.jungleredwriters.com

Inkspot:   www.midnightink.blogspot.com

Murderati:   www.murderati.com

Murder by 4:   www.murderby4.blogspot.com

Predators & Editors:   www.anotherealm.com.predators

The Outfit, A Collective of Chicago Crime Writers: www.theoutfitcollective.blogspot.com

The Mystery Short Story Web Log Project: www.criminalbrief.com (Now archived; many of these bloggers have migrated to Sleuth Sayers, www.sleuthsayers.blogspot.com)

Women of Mystery: www.womenofmystery.net

# About the Contributors:

**Jeanne M. Dams** writes two series, the Dorothy Martin series featuring the retired American schoolteacher living in England and another about amateur sleuth Hilda Johansson, a young immigrant from Sweden working as a servant in turn-of-the-19th-century in South Bend. She has published 18 novels. *Murder in Burnt Orange* was published in 2011 and *The Evil Men Do* is due in the U.S. in 2012.

**Phil Dunlap** is a longtime journalist, freelance writer, and author. Over the years he has been a correspondent for the *Indianapolis Star*, plus writing numerous articles for *Indiana Business, Plane & Pilot Magazine, Sport Aviation, The Good Old Days, The Christian Herald*, and many other regional and local publications. *Saving Mattie* won the 2009 Eppie Award for Best Traditional Western in its eBook version. *Ambush Creek*, part of the Piedmont Kelly series, was published in 2010 and the start of a new series, *Cotton's War*, in 2011.

Author of nine novels, **Michael Dymmoch** has served as president and secretary of the Midwest chapter of Mystery Writers of America, and newsletter editor for the Chicagoland chapter of Sisters in Crime. *M.I.A.* is her latest novel. Michael lives and writes in Chicago.

After discovering the works of Dick Francis, **Kit Ehrman** quit her government job and went to work in the horse industry. Twenty-five years later, Ehrman combined her love of horses and mysteries by penning the award-winning, equine-oriented mystery series featuring barn manager and amateur sleuth Steve Cline. Published by Poisoned Pen Press, the series has received numerous awards and outstanding reviews in *The New York Times, Publishers Weekly, Library Journal, Booklist, Kirkus, The Denver Post*, and the *Chicago Tribune* among others. Her latest is *Triple Cross*, published in 2007, which is the fourth in the series.

**Terence Faherty** is the Indianapolis-based author of two mystery series, the Shamus-winning Scott Elliott private eye series, set in Hollywood, and the Edgar-nominated Owen Keane series, which follows the adventures of a failed seminarian turned metaphysical detective. His work has been reissued in the United Kingdom, Japan, Italy, and Germany. Two additions to the Scott Elliott series, *Dance in the Dark* and *The Hollywood Op*, a collection of short stories, were published in 2011.

**S. M. Harding** has taught grade and high school, owned her own store in Chicago and retreat center in New Mexico, been a college professor of design, photography, and philosophy, and a chef. She's had close to twenty short mystery stories published in a number of anthologies and mystery magazines. Among the most recent are "Warriors Know Their Duty" in *Murder to Mil-Spec* (Wolfmont Press), and "Snake in the Grass" and "Under the Tree of Life" in *Spinetingler*.

**Libby Fischer Hellmann** writes two series. Her 5th novel, *Easy Innocence*, introduced PI and former cop Georgia Davis. Her other 4-book series features video producer and single mother Ellie Foreman. Hellmann's sixth novel, *Doubleback*, (October, Bleak House Books) pairs both protagonists in a thriller that begins in Chicago but ends in the high desert of Southern Arizona. In addition, Poisoned Pen Press is re-releasing *An Image of Death*, Hellmann's third novel which also features both characters. Libby has published over 12 short stories and has edited the acclaimed crime fiction anthology, *Chicago Blues*. She lives in the Chicago area.

**Jim Huang** owned The Mystery Company in Carmel, Indiana, and is the publisher of Crum Creek Press. Three non-fiction books Jim's edited have been nominated for the Anthony, Macavity, Edgar, and Agatha Awards. He also served on the national board of Sisters in Crime.

**Dana Kaye Litoff** received her B.A. in Fiction Writing from Columbia College Chicago. After college, she worked as a freelance writer and book critic. Her work has appeared in the Chicago Sun-Times, Time Out Chicago, Crimespree Magazine, Windy City Times, Bitch Magazine, and on GapersBlock.com. She's a publicist, specializing in arts clientele.

Raised in the Cascade Mountains of Oregon, **William Kent Krueger** briefly attended Stanford University – before being kicked out for radical activities. After that, he logged timber, worked construction, tried his hand at free-lance journalism, and eventually ended up researching child development at the University of Minnesota. He writes a mystery series set in the north woods of Minnesota. His protagonist is Cork O'Connor, the former sheriff of Tamarack County and a man of mixed heritage – part Irish and part Ojibwe. His work has received a number of awards including the Minnesota Book Award, the Loft-McKnight Fiction Award, the Anthony Award, the Barry Award, and the Friends of American Writers Prize. The eleventh book in his series, *Northwest Angle*, appeared in

2011. He does all his creative writing in a little St. Paul coffee shop whose identity he prefers to keep secret.

**Beverle Graves Myers** enjoys mixing murder, music and intrigue in her Tito Amato/Baroque Mystery series set in 18th-century Venice. This Kentucky author also writes short fiction which has appeared in *Alfred Hitchcock Mystery Magazine, Woman's World*, and numerous other magazines and anthologies. Her work has been nominated for the Macavity, Derringer, and Kentucky Literary awards.

**Tony Perona's** series features Nick Bertetto, a freelance writer and stay-at-home dad in Indianapolis. The third in the series, *Saintly Remains*, was published in 2009. Tony Perona is a former General Motors advertising/public relations manager who became the first man at GM to use the corporation's two-year leave-of-absence policy to care for his children. While at home Tony kept up his writing skills by becoming a newspaper correspondent and column- ist. When the company could not reinstate him, he opened Tony Perona Writing to service the public relations needs of other companies. His interest in mystery fiction led him to create novels featuring stay-at-home dad/former investiga- tive reporter Nick Bertetto. Tony is also the co-editor of an anthology of short mysteries involving the Indianapolis 500, a natural for him since he grew up in Speedway, Indiana a few blocks from the track.

**Mary Saums** worked as a recording engineer in her youth in Muscle Shoals on albums by Bob Dylan, Roy Orbison, Jimmy Buffett and many other fine artists. Her first mystery series featured singer Willi Taft and began with *Midnight Hour*. Her new series stars two gun-toting ladies in their sixties, Jane Thistle, smart and British, and Phoebe Twigg, completely Southern. They made their debut in *Thistle and Twigg*, which was a finalist for the 2008 SIBA Award for Fiction, presented by the Southeastern Independent Booksellers Association. The second book, *Mighty Old Bones*, was a Romantic Times Top Pick. Mary's short story "Run Don't Run" appears in the anthology *Blues*, an October 2009 release.

**Sharon Short** is the author of the Stain-Busting mystery series with Josie Toadfern, laundromat owner and amateur sleuth. The most recent adventure is chronicled in *Tie Dyed and Dead*. She also writes "Sanity Check," a humor column for the *Dayton Daily News* and does occasional commentaries for WMUB, southwestern Ohio's NPR station.

**Barbara Shoup** is the author of seven novels and co-author of two books about the creative process. The recipient of numerous grants from the Indiana Arts Council, two creative renewal grants from the Arts Council of Indianapolis, and the 2006 PEN Phyllis Naylor Working Writer Fellowship, she is currently the executive director of the Writers' Center of Indiana, an associate faculty member at Indiana University-Purdue University at Indianapolis and the University of Indianapolis, and an associate editor with OV Books. She is an avid reader of mysteries.

**Mark Richard Zubro** has published twenty-one books: twelve in the Tom and Scott series, the most recent of which is *Schooled in Murder*. His other series features detective Paul Turner. The most recent book in that series is *Hook, Line, and Homicide*. He is working on a young adult novel, a first book in a private eye series, volume three of a gay space epic, and the next book in the Paul Turner series. His other interests include eating chocolate, napping, and reading. His book *A Simple Suburban Murder* won the Lambda Literary Award for Best Gay Mystery.

# Acknowledgments:

Our thanks go to Jim Huang, former owner of The Mystery Company, Carmel, Indiana, for his generous support of this project, the writing community of Indiana, and the entire mystery genre; to Marianne Halbert for her eagle-eye; and to Mark Latta for all his help in bringing this to the printed and electronic page.

CPSIA information can be obtained at www.ICGtesting.com
Printed in the USA
LVOW01s1139271013

358775LV00001B/104/P

9 780984 950102